Functional Analysis

A Practitioner's Guide to Implementation and Training

Critical Specialties in Treating Autism and Other Behavioral Challenges

Series Editor
Jonathan Tarbox

Functional Analysis
A Practitioner's Guide to Implementation and Training

James T. Chok
West Chester, PA, United States

Jill M. Harper
Andover, MA, United States

Mary Jane Weiss
Andover, MA, United States

Frank L. Bird
Andover, MA, United States

James K. Luiselli
Andover, MA, United States

ACADEMIC PRESS
An imprint of Elsevier

ELSEVIER

Academic Press is an imprint of Elsevier
125 London Wall, London EC2Y 5AS, United Kingdom
525 B Street, Suite 1650, San Diego, CA 92101, United States
50 Hampshire Street, 5th Floor, Cambridge, MA 02139, United States
The Boulevard, Langford Lane, Kidlington, Oxford OX5 1GB, United Kingdom

Copyright © 2020 Elsevier Inc. All rights reserved.

No part of this publication may be reproduced or transmitted in any form or by any means, electronic or mechanical, including photocopying, recording, or any information storage and retrieval system, without permission in writing from the publisher. Details on how to seek permission, further information about the Publisher's permissions policies and our arrangements with organizations such as the Copyright Clearance Center and the Copyright Licensing Agency, can be found at our website: www.elsevier.com/permissions.

This book and the individual contributions contained in it are protected under copyright by the Publisher (other than as may be noted herein).

Notices
Knowledge and best practice in this field are constantly changing. As new research and experience broaden our understanding, changes in research methods, professional practices, or medical treatment may become necessary.

Practitioners and researchers must always rely on their own experience and knowledge in evaluating and using any information, methods, compounds, or experiments described herein. In using such information or methods they should be mindful of their own safety and the safety of others, including parties for whom they have a professional responsibility.

To the fullest extent of the law, neither the Publisher nor the authors, contributors, or editors, assume any liability for any injury and/or damage to persons or property as a matter of products liability, negligence or otherwise, or from any use or operation of any methods, products, instructions, or ideas contained in the material herein.

British Library Cataloguing-in-Publication Data
A catalogue record for this book is available from the British Library

Library of Congress Cataloging-in-Publication Data
A catalog record for this book is available from the Library of Congress

ISBN: 978-0-12-817212-4

For Information on all Academic Press publications
visit our website at https://www.elsevier.com/books-and-journals

Publisher: Nikki Levy
Acquisition Editor: Joslyn Chaiprasert-Paguio
Editorial Project Manager: Barbara Makinster
Production Project Manager: Paul Prasad Chandramohan
Cover Designer: Mark Rogers

Typeset by MPS Limited, Chennai, India

CONTENTS

About the authors vii
Series foreword: Critical specialties in treating autism and other
behavioral challenges ix
Preface xi

Chapter 1 Introduction to functional analysis 1
1.1 Historical overview 1
1.2 Standard functional analysis methodology 3
1.3 Safety considerations 4
1.4 Training considerations 5
1.5 Medical considerations 6
1.6 Summary 6

Chapter 2 Conducting standard functional analysis sessions 9
2.1 Overview of training procedures 9
2.2 Conducting standard functional analysis sessions 15
2.3 Reproducible figures and forms 25

**Chapter 3 Conducting functional analysis sessions with children
and adults** 27
3.1 Overview of training procedures 27
3.2 Practicing standard functional analysis sessions with children
and adults 28
3.3 Reproducible figures and forms 31

Chapter 4 Extending standard functional analysis conditions 39
4.1 Overview of training procedures 39
4.2 Developing unique functional analysis conditions 40
4.3 Reproducible figures and forms 47

Chapter 5 Measurement, experimental design, methodology 55
5.1 Overview of training procedures 55
5.2 Measurement 56
5.3 Experimental designs 59

5.4 Methodology 60
5.5 Reproducible figures and forms.. 68

**Chapter 6 Graphing, graph interpretation, managing
           undifferentiated data 79**
6.1 Overview of training procedures... 79
6.2 Graphing 85
6.3 Reproducible figures for graphing 87
6.4 Graph interpretation.. 88
6.5 Reproducible figures for graph interpretation 109
6.6 Managing undifferentiated data 110
6.7 Reproducible figures for managing undifferentiated data......... 118

Chapter 7 Supervision and mentoring.. 123
7.1 Overview of training procedures... 123
7.2 Reproducible figures and forms.. 126

References 137
Index 141

ABOUT THE AUTHORS

James T. Chok, PhD, BCBA-D is a licensed psychologist, neuropsychologist, and Board Certified Behavior Analyst. Dr. Chok received his doctoral degree from the University of North Carolina at Greensboro and completed a 1-year internship and a 2-year postdoctoral fellowship in neuropsychology at McLean Hospital/Harvard Medical School. Dr. Chok previously served as the Senior Director of Clinical Services for the Residential Treatment Facility at Melmark Pennsylvania, which specializes in the treatment of individuals with autism spectrum disorder, intellectual disability, and severe challenging behavior. He now maintains a private practice in West Chester, PA, specializing in diagnostic assessments and the treatment of OCD, panic disorder, and other anxiety disorders. Dr. Chok previously served as the Vice President of the New Hampshire chapter of the International OCD Foundation and is currently President of the Pennsylvania Association of Behavior Analysis.

Jill M. Harper, PhD, BCBA-D, LBA is a Board Certified Behavior Analyst and licensed behavior analyst. She is the Director of Professional Development, Clinical Training, and Research at Melmark New England and holds an adjunct faculty position with Endicott College. Her research interests include the assessment and treatment of severe behavior disorders, mechanisms responsible for behavior change, and organizational behavior management. Dr. Harper has published her work in several peer-reviewed journals such as the *Journal of Applied Behavior Analysis* and the *Journal of Developmental and Physical Disabilities* and regularly presents at regional and national conferences.

Mary Jane Weiss, PhD, BCBA-D, LBA is a licensed clinical psychologist, a Board Certified Behavior Analyst, and a licensed behavior analyst. She is the Director of Programs in Applied Behavior Analysis at Endicott College, where she oversees the PhD in ABA and the master's programs in ABA and in Autism and ABA. At Melmark, she is a Senior Director of Research. Dr. Weiss is a regular presenter at national conferences and publishes frequently on ABA and its application to individuals with ASD. She is on the Board of Association for Science in Autism Treatment, is an advisor to the Cambridge Center for Behavioral Studies, serves on the Scientific Council of the Organization for Autism Research, is on the Professional Advisory Board of Autism New Jersey, and is a regular contributor to the ABA Ethics Hotline.

Frank L. Bird, MEd, BCBA is the Vice President and Chief Clinical Officer for Melmark Inc. He has served this role for the past 12 years, and his primary responsibilities include developing and overseeing Melmark's clinical foundation, ensuring integrity across programs, establishing clinical resources, mentoring young clinicians and educators, and strategically planning for organizational and clinical growth. He received his Board Certified Behavior Analyst certification in 2000 and has been practicing applied behavior analysis in community-based settings in Massachusetts and Pennsylvania for 40 years. He has an extended history of developing clinical support systems for challenging behaviors for children and adults with the diagnosis of autism, acquired brain injury, dual diagnosis, and mental illness. His demonstrated abilities include clinical design, staff development, research and training, program development, and systems analysis. Frank has been responsible for developing over 80 programs in support of individuals with disabilities over the course of his career.

James K. Luiselli, EdD, ABPP, BCBA-D is a licensed psychologist, diplomat in cognitive and behavioral psychology, and Board Certified Behavior Analyst. He currently serves as the Director of Clinical Development and Research at Melmark New England and Adjunct Faculty within the School Psychology Program at William James College. Dr. Luiselli has published 16 books, 50 book chapters, and more than 260 journal articles in the areas of applied behavior analysis, organizational behavior management, performance improvement, professional training, and clinical practice. He is an Associate Editor for the *Journal of Child and Family Studies* and serves on the Board of Editors for several other journals such as *Education and Treatment of Children*, *Journal of Developmental and Physical Disabilities*, *Advances in Neurodevelopmental Disorders*, and *Mindfulness*.

Series foreword: Critical specialties in treating autism and other behavioral challenges

Purpose

The purpose of this series is to provide treatment manuals that address topics of high importance to practitioners working with individuals with autism spectrum disorders (ASD) and other behavioral challenges. This series offers targeted books that focus on particular clinical problems that have not been sufficiently covered in recent books and manuals. This series includes books that directly address clinical specialties that are simultaneously high prevalence (i.e., every practitioner faces these problems at some point) and yet are also commonly known to be a major challenge, for which most clinicians do not possess sufficient specialized training. The authors of individual books in this series are top-tier experts in their respective specialties. The books in this series will help to solve the problems that practitioners face by taking the very best in practical knowledge from the leading experts in each specialty and making it readily available in a consumable, practical format. The overall goal of this series is to provide useful information that clinicians can immediately put into practice. The primary audience for this series is professionals who work in treatment and education for individuals with ASD and other behavioral challenges. These professionals include Board Certified Behavior Analysts, Speech and Language Pathologists, Licensed Marriage and Family Therapists, Licensed clinical psychologist, and special education teachers. Although not the primary audience for this series, parents and family members of individuals with ASD will find the practical information contained in this series highly useful.

Jonathan Tarbox, is the Program Director of the Master of Science in Applied Behavior Analysis program at the University of Southern California, as well as Director of Research at FirstSteps for Kids.

Dr. Tarbox is the Editor of the *Journal Behavior Analysis in Practice* and serves on the editorial boards of multiple scientific journals related to autism and behavior analysis. He has published four books on autism treatment and well over 70 peer-reviewed journal articles and chapters in scientific texts. His research focuses on behavioral interventions for teaching complex skills to individuals with autism, treatment of feeding disorders, and the application of Acceptance and Commitment Therapy to applied behavior analysis.

Series Editor
Jonathan Tarbox, PhD, BCBA-D
University of Southern California, Los Angeles,
CA, United States
FirstSteps for Kids

PREFACE

The seminal publication on functional analysis (FA) methodology by Iwata, Dorsey, Slifer, Bauman, and Richman (1982/1994) has generated hundreds of studies documenting the contribution of FA to intervention formulation and implementation (Beavers, Iwata, & Lerman, 2013; Call, Scheithauer, & Mevers, 2017). Indeed, conducting FA to inform intervention decisions is a critical practice standard for behavior analysts within educational and treatment settings serving children, youth, and adults. Further, the *Professional and Ethical Compliance Code for Behavior Analysts* [Behavior Analyst Certification Board (BACB), 2017] emphasizes functional assessment, including FA, before developing behavior reduction plans. Conducting an FA of challenging behavior is also an application priority in the BACB Task List for board certified behavior analysts (BCBA) and board certified assistant behavior analysts (BCaBA).

Despite the acknowledged benefits and practice mandates, many behavior analysts and other behavioral practitioners may have limited training and experience conducting FA and evaluating–interpreting findings. Equally important is a practitioner's knowledge about and adherence to critical ethical principles and guidelines which apply when planning and conducting FA. Another concern is that numerous adaptations and revisions have been made to the originally reported FA methodology—keeping pace with these developments is not easy for practitioners who do not read or have difficulty accessing the evidence-based research literature. Note too that even FA-experienced and competent behavior analysts do not have readily available training curricula for instructing less knowledgeable practitioners, supervisees, and students. Finally, there are many procedural exigencies that can affect the outcomes from FA but are not explained in publications or included within conventional training.

Functional Analysis: A Practitioner's Guide to Implementation and Training addresses the previously cited concerns about conducting and training FA. One focus of the book is providing practitioners with the most updated information about applying the wide span of current FA methodologies, which are geared specifically to applied service settings. In this capacity the book will serve as a self-instructional guide. The second primary focus of the book is giving practitioners a curriculum for teaching FA implementation to a broad-base of trainees and careproviders within schools, clinics, centers, and human services organizations. We anticipate that this breadth of coverage will appeal to a large audience of behavior analysts, behavioral psychologists, and behavior specialists who are responsible for conducting and training FA within their practice domains.

Each chapter in the book represents a designated training level. Chapters 2–5 begin with an Overview of Training Procedures specific to the level, a Summary of Training Steps, and Criteria to Pass the level requirements. These chapters include presentation graphics in the form of PowerPoint slides with "notes to the trainer" that can be freely accessed and downloaded through the publisher's website. The concluding section of these chapters is Reproducible Figures and Forms such as data recording sheets, rating scales, quizzes, and other level-specific documents. Chapter 1, Introduction to functional analysis, Chapter 6, Graphing, graph interpretation, managing undifferentiated data, and Chapter 7, Supervision and mentoring, have a slightly different format based on the area and content of training.

Our curriculum emphasizes both knowledge and performance competencies. Thus trainees are taught concepts, principles, and terminology that apply to FA methodology, and the skills to implement procedures accurately. Competencies are measured throughout training to ensure that trainees demonstrate mastery at and before moving on to each level of the curriculum. Within the curriculum and chapter narrative, we use "the clinician" when referencing the person leading the FA, "the therapist" when referencing the person conducting FA sessions, and "child or adult" when referencing the person being evaluated through FA.

One topic we do not discuss is function-based intervention, that is, behavior-change plans and procedures informed by FA. It is simply beyond the scope of this book to fully detail the multifaceted process of intervention formulation and intervention derived from FA. Readers can refer to several exemplary texts that fully explore the relationship between FA and intervention (Cooper, Heron, & Heward, 2007; Kazdin, 2013; Miltenberger, 2016).

The book can be used for conducting FA with children, youth, and adults who have intellectual and developmental disabilities, psychiatric disorders, brain injury, neurocognitive deficits, and related learning and behavior challenges. As well, the training curriculum and methods encompass practitioners within multiple settings such as public and private schools, day-treatment centers, clinics, residential services programs, and community-based habilitation agencies. Indeed, a strength of FA illustrated in the book is generalizability among target populations, presenting problems, and environments.

We have paid special attention throughout the book to conducting FA safely, ethically, and with sensitivity to the unique circumstances of trainers and the individuals who receive services. Planning and implementing FA has as much to do with a practitioner's social, interpersonal, and communication skills as it does with technical expertise. Additionally, matters of culture and diversity must direct FA training and implementation, which we embrace as a dominant standard of professional practice (Fong, Catagnus, Brodhead, Quigley, & Field, 2016).

Finally, the book presents a comprehensive training curriculum that is best implemented sequentially across all levels. However, some practitioners may only want to highlight a few sections of individual chapters based on particular training objectives. Similarly, our presentation materials can be incorporated into training precisely as shown in the book or adapted in whatever format will be most effective. Like FA itself, we encourage creativity, critical thinking, and innovation when designing and instituting training, conducting analyses, and supervising the learning and practice of trainees. Our desire is that *Functional Analysis: A Practitioner's Guide to Implementation and Training* achieves these goals and contributes to professional practice.

The PowerPoint slides associated with the chapters are available on the companion site (https://www.elsevier.com/books-and-journals/book-companion/9780128172124)

CHAPTER 1

Introduction to functional analysis

1.1 Historical overview

Functional assessment/analysis is a crucial element of behavior analytic practice when treating learners with ASD as well as other challenging conditions. The technology has enabled the identification of the function of challenging behavior and has distinguished the field of ABA from the antiquated behavior modification approach. Instead of simply reducing the extent to which behaviors pose interference, clinicians now seek to understand why such behaviors arise and persist, and endeavor to change the environment in ways that make such behaviors less relevant and less likely.

FA involves the systematic manipulations of environmental variables to identify those that contribute to the maintenance of challenging behavior. The most cited article in reference to FA methodology is Iwata et al. (1982/1994). A review of the literature leading up to this seminal article is presented below.

Bijou, Peterson, and Ault (1968) first proposed the integration of descriptive and experimental analysis of behavior. The authors proposed the use of descriptive data to inform experimental evaluations. In essence, Bijou et al. set forth the proposal for the later development of formalized FA methodology, "Descriptive studies provide information only on events and their occurrence. They do not provide information on the functional properties of events or the functional relationships among events. Experimental studies provide that kind of information" (pp. 176−177).

In 1964 Allen et al. published the first empirical demonstration of the systematic introduction and withdrawal of social attention. The participant, a young girl, interacted primarily with adults within her environment. To increase peer interaction, adult attention was delivered contingent upon peer interaction and was withheld when she was playing alone or seeking adult attention. Peer interaction increased to high levels when adult attention followed peer interaction and decreased to baseline levels when adult interaction was provided noncontingently.

In 1969 Lovaas and Simmons systematically evaluated attention as a potential controlling variable of the self-injurious behavior of three participants. Attention extinction resulted in large reductions of self-injurious behavior across all three participants, which demonstrated that attention was at least one controlling variable in the maintenance of this behavior for two of the three participants. Due to the initial increase in challenging behavior (self-injury in this case) that is often observed with the implementation of extinction, the authors evaluated a punishment procedure (electric shock) for two of the three participants for whom continued self-injury would place the participant at risk.

Schaefer (1970) provided a systematic replication of these basic procedures when investigating the shaping of what approximated head hitting and aggression (hitting paw against the side of the cage). Using food reinforcement, Schaefer shaped these two responses in rhesus monkeys in an operant chamber. This work provided further empirical evidence of the potential impact of contingent consequences on certain behavioral repertoires, strengthening the confidence that specific behaviors are a function of their consequences.

Carr (1977) extended the systematic manipulation of environmental variables beyond positive reinforcement in the form of attention. This study examined social attention, access to tangibles, escape form aversive events, and sensory stimulation as potential controlling variables of self-injurious behavior. In this study the range of environmental variables that could influence behavior was expanded and included a variety of consequences commonly associated with challenging behaviors. Carr's work foreshadowed the development of the standard FA methodology, focusing on the explicit manipulation of consequences that might be responsible for the maintenance of behavior. Behavior analysts began viewing assessment as a way to determine the function of a behavior, that is, as a means to understanding why the behavior had evolved and was maintained in the individual's behavioral repertoire. With this focus on environmental variables as an explanation for behavior, the ability to influence and control such behavior with environmental adjustments was conceptually crystalized.

1.2 Standard functional analysis methodology

Iwata et al. (1982/1994) demonstrated how a formalized protocol could be used to determine the maintaining variables or functions of behavior. Session duration and other elements of the protocol were made uniform. The authors operationally defined and technologically described a technology for assessing the impact of each function. The study both tested the implementation of the protocol to evaluate the function of behavior and affirmed the concept that behavior is a function of its consequences.

In a brilliant variation of procedure, these researchers contingently applied hypothesized maintaining variables when challenging behavior occurred. Comparing the rates of behavior across conditions, it was possible to identify environmental factors associated with higher rates of the behavior. From an experimental perspective, it allowed for the isolation of individual variables. Trainers could now see how attention influenced the target behavior or how escape from demands influenced the target behavior.

The technology was unique, and a bit clinically counterintuitive. It was also extremely powerful, revealing associations between environmental factors and behavior at an unprecedented level of clarity. The study literally revolutionized how behavior was conceptualized and how assessment would be done. It also brought a new set of ethical considerations. Reinforcing challenging behavior, in and of itself, was unusual and posed several risks important in implementation. In addition the skill set itself of conducting the FA emerged as a new competency, requiring comprehensive training and ongoing supervision. In the decades since this study the standard FA technology has stood the test of time, has been empirically validated in dozens of studies, and has emerged as the gold standard approach in the assessment and treatment of severe challenging behavior. Ethical considerations with the approach are now well understood and are crucial for the safe and effective use of FA procedures.

Several overarching themes are essential to the ethical, safe, and effective practice of FA. These considerations include establishing a safe and humane assessment and treatment environment, providing adequate training and supervision to staff conducting such procedures, and collaborating with medical personnel to address the biological variables and considerations that require attention in the process of FA and treatment development.

1.3 Safety considerations

The most important consideration is the use of procedures that are safe, humane, and appropriate to the context and behavioral presentation. As the field has evolved, many procedures are available for conducting a functional assessment/FA. Some procedures pose more risk inherently (e.g., FAs), as they are designed to evoke more challenging behaviors in contrived contexts. Within these procedures, variations have emerged which limit risk. For example, a latency-based FA (in which the session is terminated after the first instance of the target behavior) poses less physical risk than a traditional FA (in which frequency of the target behavior would be the measure). A latency-based FA might be selected when the presenting behaviors are dangerous, such as in the case of self-injury or aggression.

In addition, sessions may be altered to reduce risk in other ways, including the shortening of sessions. Effective assessments have been demonstrated with sessions as brief as 2 minutes of 5 minutes, as compared with a traditional session length of 10 or more minutes. Similarly, risk may be reduced by adding protective equipment for the client and for the clinicians, reducing the physical harm posed by the behaviors themselves.

At times, the team may decide that an FA is too unsafe, and they may target other behaviors or use indirect procedures. For example, an assessment may target precursor behaviors. In this way, the behavior itself may be prevented, and the assessment may focus on behaviors earlier in the chain. Alternately, the assessment might focus on a replacement skill such as an "functional communication response" (FCR). A trainer might examine which FCR is more likely to occur in controlled conditions, lending support to a hypothesis regarding function in a slightly different manner. Finally, the team might elect to do an indirect assessment that does not involve environmental manipulation and may infer function from the use of indirect or naturalistic assessments only. While this is not preferred and is not as accurate as FA procedures, it may be the safest and most efficient method and is occasionally the best option.

As with other elements of behavior analytic practice, individualization is the gold standard and a defining feature of good practice. FA is a complex skill set, and it is designed to treat the most complex challenging behaviors encountered by professional trainers. The FA skill set is nuanced and highly individualized and requires care and diligence in application.

1.4 Training considerations

As indicated above, FA is a complex procedure that poses inherent risk. Trainers must be honest about their level of competence and mindful about their need for assistance in designing and implementing FAs. A hallmark ethical principle guiding the practice of trainers is to practice only within the boundaries of one's competence. Put simply, trainers do only what they know how to do and do not engage in professional activities for which they lack training, supervised experience, and clinical competence. This is important in the content of FA, especially because of the risks posed by the procedures.

Trainers must continually examine the extent to which their competence matches the clinical needs of a child or adult and other elements of the treatment challenge. If there is a need for additional expertise, a trainer should voice this concern and request additional resources, supports, or consultation.

Organizations conducting FA must support trainers in attaining and maintaining clinical competency and in securing additional training and supports when they are needed. In addition, comprehensive training should be provided to staff members who will be required/expected to conduct FA.

Training should include both conceptual and practice elements, and trainers should be supported in the actual implementation challenges of conducting FA. Our curriculum is designed with this ultimate skill set in mind and provides detailed exercises in conducting experimental FA. Organizations are encouraged to train and supervise the development of an FA skill set, to encourage mentorship among trainers in the setting, and to continually query staff members about their readiness for and comfort with conducting such assessments.

Supervision is a special concern, and staff members should be assessed for competency before implementing FA procedures. It is also essential that trainers closely monitor the implementation of the procedures and the medical and behavioral state of the adult or child participant during the assessment.

1.5 Medical considerations

When planning and conducting FA, trainers should collaborate with medical professionals about health concerns and possible medical explanations for the emergence or worsening of challenging behavior. It is not uncommon for challenging behavior to emerge as a result of physical pain or discomfort. For example the presence of an ear infection may occasion self-injury. Seasonal allergies might predispose an individual to aggression. Muscular injury might contribute to noncompliance and a reluctance to engage in mobile tasks. As with any individual, the interface between biology and behavior is a complex interaction. Understanding the contribution of physiological states and processes to challenging behavior is an additional skill set and requires interdisciplinary assessment and collaboration.

It is particularly important that medical considerations be considered when challenging behaviors are new, when behaviors have suddenly worsened, or when recurring behavioral patterns are likely (e.g., seasonal variations). Trainers have an obligation to assess for such comorbid conditions and to ensure that they are fully treated as part of a comprehensive plan. This should be done as part of a comprehensive assessment and should precede the development of a plan to formally assess or to intervene.

There are also medical considerations for the assessment itself. The occurrence of challenging behaviors is likely during any FA, even when the methods used are selected for the reduced occurrences associated with the particular method (e.g., latency-based FA). Medical risk should be a consideration in the selection of the procedure and should be discussed by the entire team. Furthermore, medical personnel should be consulted about the need for and use of protective equipment during any assessment procedures and as part of an intervention package. In addition the presence of medical personnel during an FA may be needed to assess physical injury, to monitor the physical impact of behaviors in the moment, and to alter or terminate sessions for medical reasons.

1.6 Summary

FA methodology demonstrated functional relations between environmental variables and behaviors. It revolutionized the treatment of challenging behaviors and clearly proved that behaviors could be influenced and even controlled by changes in environmental conditions. Early behavior analysts demonstrated the ability to reduce challenging behaviors and increase social behaviors through the contingent use of attention. Carr (1977) expanded the range of environmental variables assessed for their impact on rates of challenging behaviors, to include tangible, escape, and sensory stimulation. Iwata et al. (1982/1994) utilized what has become known as the standard FA methodology to systematically assess the contingent effects of these consequences. Many variations of the FA methodology allow for increased and nuanced individualization in the assessment process. The skill set associated with conducting FAs is complex, requiring substantial training and rigorous oversight and supervision. Medical concerns must be addressed during the preassessment and FA. Safety considerations are of paramount importance and must be at the forefront of the trainer's concerns. FA is a powerful technology, with great potential for improving the outcomes associated with behavior analytic intervention. Safeguards are important to ensure competent and safe use.

The identification and use of safe and effective procedures are the goal for any behavior analytic practice context, and FA is no exception. The technology has evolved in exciting, innovative, and specialized directions, adding significantly to the effectiveness of our efforts to understand and to treat the most challenging behaviors. Effective treatment follows from assessments that are well-designed, appropriate to the presenting context, and aligned with best practice guidelines.

It is important for individuals and for organizations to commit to safe and thorough implementation of FAs. In the context of safety, variations of FA procedures that reduce risk should be considered. Staff must be trained and supervised in the procedures to reduce risk to client and to staff. Medical professionals should be consulted about the behaviors themselves and about the procedures that should be used to ensure safety within the sessions.

The technology of FA is powerful and has enabled much more effective intervention at the level of the individual. Behavior analysis' strength is in the individual application of the science, and the tool kit of FA is a stellar example of how individualization can lead to efficient and effective treatment. With proper attention to the safe and ethically sound implementation of this technology, socially significant changes are closer at hand than ever before, and our ultimate outcomes for each learner are more readily attainable.

CHAPTER 2

Conducting standard functional analysis sessions

2.1 Overview of training procedures

This level of the curriculum is designed to help trainees become more comfortable conducting standard functional analysis (FA) sessions. Training begins with an interactive slideshow presentation describing the key features of each type of FA condition. As each condition is described, trainees have the opportunity to practice the basic components of each session with the trainer. Some materials are needed to carry out this portion of the curriculum, such as work materials for the escape condition, toys for the attention and play conditions, and leisure items for the tangible condition. Trainers model the main components of each condition, including arranging the environment, beginning the session, responding to the target behavior, and ignoring nontarget behavior. Trainees then volunteer to practice these basic components. Trainers provide feedback along the way to reinforce correct responding and clarify incorrect responding.

Once the trainer has covered each standard FA condition in this manner, trainees should have a basic understanding of how to setup the environment for each condition and conduct standard FA sessions. A round robin activity is introduced next in order to promote generalization and the flexible use of these skills. During this activity, trainees randomly select a condition to practice, along with an operational definition for a challenging behavior. Thus, trainees need to be ready to practice any of the conditions on the spot and respond to varying challenging behaviors which are emitted by the trainee playing the role of the child or adult in a nonscripted manner (i.e., the trainee decides when to emit the challenging behavior and the form of nontarget behavior emitted is his or her choice). The trainer will take performance data on the trainee who will play the role of the session therapist, while another trainee plays the role of a child or adult with challenging behavior. Trainees are assessed on their ability to arrange the environment correctly, state the correct discriminative stimulus (S^D), provide the appropriate consequence when the target behavior is emitted, and ignore distracter behavior. Results for each trainee are documented on the *data sheet for round robin practice sessions*, which is displayed in Fig. 2.1. Trainees need to successfully demonstrate all of these skills with 100% integrity during a trial for each of the five standard FA conditions (attention, escape, play, tangible, alone). Trials should last about 1 minute so that there is enough time for trainee to respond to both challenging and distracting behavior.

After the Round Robin activity has been completed, trainees will practice conducting full simulated sessions in which each of the four social conditions are carried out according to a script. These scripted sessions standardize the training process for each trainee so that they are equally responding to the same number of target and nontarget behaviors each session. The length of each script is 5 minutes, which better approximates the session length when conditions with children and adults are carried out. Scripts for each condition are displayed in Figs. 2.2–2.5. Performance data are recorded on the *simulated condition feedback forms* (Figs. 2.6–2.9). A summary of each trainee's performance across each of the social conditions is documented on the *performance summary sheet for simulated conditions* (Fig. 2.10). The *task analysis for training-simulated conditions*, displayed in Fig. 2.11, provides trainers with step-by-step instructions for completing this portion of the curriculum. Once the performance criteria are met by the trainees, they will work with the trainer on arranging a time to conduct FA sessions with children and adults, which is covered in the next chapter. A summary of the training steps, along with the criteria to pass this level, are presented next.

Training steps for Level 2
1. Trainer completes an interactive slideshow training which includes brief demonstrations of each FA condition.
2. A Round Robin series of role-play exercises is conducted, and performance of each trainee is tracked with the *data sheet for round robin practice sessions*—Fig. 2.1; each trainee must score 100% for each standard FA condition before moving on in the training.
3. Trainer conducts training of simulated FA sessions by using a standardized script for each condition
    a. Follow the *task analysis for training-simulated conditions*, Fig. 2.11, to guide you through this portion of the curriculum.

Data Sheet for Round Robin Practice Sessions

Date: _____

Staff Member	FA Condition	Correct arrangement of antecedent	Correct S^d	Correct consequence for target	Ignores distracter	Trial Passed (100% integrity)

Figure 2.1 Data sheet for round robin practice sessions.

Target Behavior: Self injurious behavior (open-handed hits to head or bites to wrist)

:05	Slap side of head w/ right hand
:10	Bang knee on bottom of table
:15	Three open ended hits to head
:55	Double hand table bang with fists
1:10	Aggress on staff slap one of their arms
1:50	Squeeze head with fists and close eyes for 5 sec
2:10	Aggress on staff with hit to arm
2:20	Bite to right wrist for 3 sec
2:30	Slap side of head w/ right hand
3:00	Double elbow bang to table
3:10	Bite to right wrist for 3 sec
3:20	Two open handed hits to head
3:30	Bite to wrist for 3 sec
4:05	Swipe materials off of table
4:15	Two open handed hits to head
4:25	One open handed hit to head
4:30	Put head down on table for 10 sec

Figure 2.2 FA script for attention condition. FA, Functional analysis.

Target Behavior: Self injurious behavior (open-handed hits to head or bites to wrists)

:00-:10	Doing work
:10	Swipes materials off of table
:20	Two open handed hits to head
:30	One open handed hit to head
:40	Put head down on table
:50 – :55	Lifts head back up and orients to task
1:10	Three open handed hits to head
1:20	Squeeze head with fists and close eyes for 5 sec
1:50	Bang knee on bottom table
2:05	Bite to right wrist for 3 sec
2:15	Slap side of head w/ right hand
2:30	Double hand table bang with fists
2:35 – 2:40	Ignore instruction
2:40 – 2:45	Ignore instruction
3:00	Aggress on staff slap one of their arms
3:10	Aggress on staff with hit to arm
3:20	Slap side of head w/ right hand
4:00	Double elbow bang to table
4:10	Bite to wrist for 3 sec
4:20	Two open handed hits to head
4:25	Bite to wrist for 3 sec

Figure 2.3 FA script for escape condition. FA, Functional analysis.

Target Behavior: Self injurious behavior (open-handed hits to head or bites to wrists)

:05	Swipe materials off table
:10	Bite to wrist for 3 sec
:30	Bite to wrist for 3 sec
:50	Double hand table bang with fists
1:10	Aggress on staff slap one of their arms
1:15	Make eye contact and say, "Help please"
1:30	Hit side of head with both hands
1:35	Bite wrist for 3 sec
1:50	Squeeze head with fists and close eyes for 5 sec
2:10	One open handed hit to head
2:15	Hit side of head with both hands
2:30	Put head down on table
2:35	Kick table
2:55	Bite to right wrist for 3 sec
3:15	Bite wrist for 1 sec
3:20	Aggress on staff with kick to leg
3:35	Hand a toy to the staff member and play for 5 sec
3:50	Double elbow bang to table
4:05	Slap side of head w/ right hand

Figure 2.4 FA script for play condition. FA, Functional analysis.

Target Behavior: Self injurious behavior (open-handed hits to head or bites to wrist)

-1:00	Play with toys appropriately
:10	Slap the table with both hands 3x
:15	Hit side of head with hand
:30	Scream for 2 sec
1:00	Bang knee against table
1:10	Bite wrist
1:25	Slaps side of head
1:35	Kick staff member
2:05	Slaps side of head
2:45	Bites wrist
2:55	Kicks desk
3:15	Slaps side of head
3:25	Screams for 3 sec
3:45	Slaps side of head with one hand
3:55	Bites wrist
4:25	Tries to grab materials from clinician
4:35	Signs "more" while making eye contact
4:45	Slaps side of head

Figure 2.5 FA script for tangible condition. FA, Functional analysis.

Functional Analysis

Date: _____ Trainee: _____ Trainer: _____

Attention Condition		
Correct Response	Present (+) or Absent (-)	Overall Accuracy
Client and therapist are in a room with moderately preferred items		(Out of 1)
Therapist starts timer for the session		(Out of 1)
Therapist states, "I have some work to do," picks up a book, and moves a minimum of 5 feet away from the client		(Out of 1)
Therapist delivers 3-5 s of attention (physical and verbal attention) contingent upon target behavior (per occurrence)		(Out of 9)
Walks a minimum of 5 feet away and attends to reading material after attention is provided (per occurrence)		(Out of 9)
Non-target behaviors ignored (per occurrence)		(Out of 8)
Total Accuracy = $\frac{\text{\# of "+" scores}}{\text{\# of "+" and "-" scores}}$	→	(Out of 29)

Total Accuracy ≥ 90%?   Yes   No

Figure 2.6 Standard FA condition feedback form—attention. FA, Functional analysis.

4. Once trainees meet the criteria for passing (see *performance summary sheet for simulated conditions*—Fig. 2.10), they move onto Level 3 of the training curriculum
5. Scripts are provided for trainers to use to simulate client behavior—Figs. 2.2–2.5, and feedback forms are used to score trainee performance—Figs. 2.6–2.9.

Criteria to pass Level 2

- Score of 100% on one trial *each* of the standard conditions (attention, escape, play, tangible, alone/ignore) during Round Robin role-play exercises
- Score of 90% or higher for the attention, escape, play, and tangible conditions during simulated sessions

Date: _____ Trainee: _____ Trainer: _____

Escape Condition		
Correct Response	Present (+) or Absent (-)	Overall Accuracy
Starts timer for session		(Out of 1)
Presents client with moderately challenging task at a continuous pace		(Out of 1)
Praises correct responses to vocal or gesture prompts (score first 10 instances)		(Out of 10)
Makes neutral statement if full physical prompt is needed for accurate response ("that's purple")		(Out of 1)
Removes task and turns away from student contingent upon target behavior		(Out of 9)
Non-target behaviors ignored		(Out of 8)
Presents task again following 20" absence of target behavior		(Out of 5)
Total Accuracy = $\frac{\text{\# of "+" scores}}{\text{\# of "+" and "-" scores}}$ →		(Out of 35)

Total Accuracy ≥ 90%?   Yes   No

Figure 2.7 Standard FA condition feedback form—escape. FA, Functional analysis.

2.2 Conducting standard functional analysis sessions

In the early 1980s, Iwata et al. (1980/1994) developed a technology for trying to understand why individuals were performing certain behaviors. This first standardized methodology for an experimental analysis of function looked at four conditions: attention, play, escape, and alone. The attention condition allows the practitioner to evaluate whether or not behavior is maintained by access to the attention provided by another individual. For example, an individual may yell out because it produces the consequence of a caregiver moving closer and interacting with the individual. The escape condition allows the practitioner to evaluate whether or not escape from aversive events is maintaining behavior. For example, yelling out may result in a caregiver removing a demand that was placed prior to the individual yelling out. The play condition serves as a control during which the individual

Date: _____   Trainee: _____   Trainer: _____

Play (FT 20" + DRA)		
Correct Response	Present (+) or Absent (-)	Overall Accuracy
Therapist starts timer for the session		(Out of 1)
Presents client with 2-3 highly preferred toys and states "here are some toys to play with"		(Out of 1)
Therapist is oriented to client, remains within 3 ft throughout the session		(Out of 1)
Responds to appropriate requests or intraverbals (per occurrence) related to attention ("Check out my car")		(Out of 2)
Ignores target behavior (per occurrence)		(Out of 8)
Total Accuracy = $\frac{\# \text{ of "+" scores}}{\# \text{ of "+" and "-" scores}}$ ⟶		(Out of 13)

Total Accuracy ≥ 90%?   Yes   No

Figure 2.8 Standard FA condition feedback form—play. FA, Functional analysis.

receives access to attention, without the presence of demands. This is an attempt to create an environment in which there is minimal to no motivation to engage in challenging behavior if it is maintained by social consequences. At times, an individual may perform a behavior for reasons other than the social consequences that follow it. For example, the behavior itself may produce reinforcing consequences (e.g., the person's yelling behavior produces an echoing sound in the hallways). Therefore, an alone condition was included in the original FA assessment to allow the practitioner to evaluate whether or not automatic reinforcement is maintaining behavior.

Functions of behavior

The purpose of an FA is to determine the type of contingency maintaining behavior. It could be a positive reinforcement contingency that is social in nature, like access to attention or providing materials. Alternatively, it may be an automatic positive reinforcement contingency, in which some sensory stimulation is occurring after the behavior that is enjoyable to the person.

Date: _____   Trainee: _____   Trainer: _____

Tangible		
Correct Response	Present (+) or Absent (-)	Overall Accuracy
Presents client with highly preferred materials for 1 min prior to session		(Out of 1)
Ignores all pre-session behaviors (appropriate and inappropriate)		(Out of 1)
Starts timer and takes away materials at start of session		(Out of 1)
Returns materials for 20" contingent upon target behavior		(Out of 7)
Takes materials away after client has not engaged in the target behavior for 20"		(Out of 7)
Ignores non-target behavior		(Out of 8)
Total Accuracy = $\frac{\text{\# of "+" scores}}{\text{\# of "+" and "-" scores}}$ ⟶		(Out of 25)

Total Accuracy ≥ 90%?   Yes   No

Figure 2.9 Standard FA condition feedback form—tangible. FA, Functional analysis.

A negative reinforcement contingency would be in effect if the reduction or removal of an aversive state occurs contingent upon behavior, such as the removal of demands following aggression. It could also be that the environment is loud and that problem behavior, such as elopement, results in a quieter environment. An automatic negative reinforcement contingency might be in effect for someone who cracks their knuckles—the behavior itself results in the reduction of something aversive (pain/tension in fingers). This process is sometimes referred to as sensory attenuation. In the next section, we will take a look at a couple of examples to help distinguish automatic positive reinforcement from automatic negative reinforcement.

Automatic negative example: cracking knuckles

Take a moment to think about the antecedent state that precedes knuckle-cracking behavior. For some, this may be described as an uncomfortable state and the consequence of knuckle cracking may reduce this discomfort. If these were the environmental conditions

18 Functional Analysis

Date: _____

Trainee: _____

Condition	Accuracy Score

Criterion to Pass:

☐ 90% or higher accuracy for each condition (Attention, Escape, Play, Tangible)

Figure 2.10 Performance summary sheet for simulated conditions.

surrounding the behavior, we would conclude that knuckle cracking is maintained by automatic negative reinforcement. With automatic negative reinforcement, the behavior itself produces an environmental change that results in a reduction in the aversive state that preceded the behavior.

Automatic positive example: jumping on a trampoline

There may also be circumstances in which the behavior itself produces pleasant consequences. For example, we may notice a child sitting in the gym with little stimulation in his or her environment. The child then begins jumping on a trampoline. We may notice the child smiling or laughing, and the child may comment that he or she is "having

Pre-Session Steps:

1) Arrange materials to be used for the Attention, Play, and Tangible sessions into piles labeled Low Preferred, Moderately Preferred, and Highly Preferred.
2) Arrange three academic tasks into the categories of Easy Demands, Moderately Difficult Demands, and Very Difficult Demands.
3) Assign one trainee to be the therapist while you, the trainer, collect treatment integrity data. Use the *Standard Functional Analysis Feedback Forms* (Figures 2.6 – 2.9) to record performance.
4) A trainee or trainer can be the actor. If the trainer is the actor, it would be helpful to have an additional trainer present to take data on the trainee's performance.

Post-Session Steps:

1) Review the performance of the therapist using the *Performance Summary Sheet for Simulated Conditions* sheet (Figure 2.11). Praise correct responding, model the correct response for any response that was inaccurate, and have the trainee practice the correct response. Answer any questions the trainee might have.
2) Rotate trainees and conditions (i.e., have the next trainee play the therapist role in a new simulated condition).
3) Randomly rearrange the toys and academic tasks into new preference piles (low/easy, moderate, high).

Continue until each trainee has achieved a score of 90% or higher for all four training conditions.

Figure 2.11 Task analysis for training-simulated conditions.

fun." If we believe that the consequences of this behavior produce pleasant consequences, we would conclude that trampoline jumping is maintained by automatic positive reinforcement. Now let's look at what changes in the environment for each of the social functions.

Attention (Sr^+)

In the attention condition, you are testing for social positive reinforcement. The environmental arrangement is deprivation from attention. Think about this as the motivating operation (MO) or establishing operation (EO). Motivating operations are either establishing the reinforcer at a higher value (establishing operations) or abolishing its reinforcing effects, in other words, making the reinforcer less valuable (abolishing operations). The initial instruction or discriminative stimulus, that signals the availability of the attention reinforcer contingent upon problem behavior, is the presence of the therapist and the statement, "Here are some toys to play with; I have some work to do." The therapist then provides the child with moderately preferred toys and diverts his or her attention to some reading materials. If the target problem behavior occurs, the therapist delivers the potential attention reinforcer in the form of a concerning statement, such as "Hey, don't do that buddy, you are going to hurt yourself," while providing 3–5 seconds of physical attention.

In this case, the therapist is giving some physical attention and brief verbal attention. The therapist immediately approaches the person to deliver this attention and then orients and walks away from them after it has been delivered. Take a moment to think about the response–reinforcer relationship. The therapist is trying to make it clear to the person that when he or she engages in the target problem behavior, the therapist will immediately and contingently provide the reinforcer. When he or she stops the behavior, the therapist will back away and cease giving attention. This approach establishes a contingency for the attention condition. Contingent means "dependent upon." In the attention condition of an FA the only way attention is provided is following the target problem behavior.

Tangible (Sr$^+$)

In the years since Iwata et al. (1980/1994) introduced the standard FA methodology, another condition which would become frequently used by clinicians and researchers, the tangible condition, was developed. The tangible condition is another test for social positive reinforcement. The way in which this condition is structured differs across research articles, so we chose what we thought was the best manner in which to do it. In this condition the client is given presession access to highly preferred items for a minute. Both target and nontarget behaviors are ignored during this presession period. Upon the start of the session, the therapist takes away the tangible items (e.g., toys, edibles, and activity), which serves as the discriminative stimulus that signals availability of the tangible reinforcer following the targeted problem behavior. Deprivation from the tangibles serves as an establishing operation (if tangibles are indeed a reinforcer). Access to tangibles would serve as an abolishing operation. Let us look at an everyday example with ice cream.

Motivating operations example: ice cream access

Take a moment to think about your motivation to work for something you love, such as ice cream. If it had been a long time since you last ate any food, in particular ice cream, and you were told, "If you complete these five checklists, you will get a bowl of ice cream," you may quickly finish the five checklists since you are in a state of deprivation from food. After you enjoy the bowl of ice cream, let us assume you are full. If someone says to you, "I'll give you another 5 checklists and you can earn ice cream again," the reinforcing effects of ice cream would be abolished because you already ate so much of it (you accessed the reinforcer and likely reached a point of satiation). Therefore, you would be less motivated to engage in the task of completing checklists.

Conducting the tangible condition

In terms of how a tangible condition is conducted, the therapist begins by providing access to tangibles during a timed presession period. At this point, the therapist is not taking data; the session has not technically started in terms of data collection. The therapist can certainly observe what is happening and take notes, but when graphing data for the session, behavior that occurs during this presession period is not included. The session starts when the tangibles are taken away. If the child or adult engages in the targeted problem behavior, the therapist returns them for a specific amount of time, such as 20 seconds. Once that period elapses, the therapist takes away the tangibles items away again and then returns them contingent upon problem behavior. This pattern is followed for the remainder of the session.

Managing additional behaviors in the tangible condition

Once the therapist begins ignoring the behaviors other than the target problem behavior, there are many scenarios for which he or she should be prepared. Let us say the problem behavior of interest is aggression. The individual may engage in a nontarget problem behavior, such as self-injurious behavior (SIB). At this point the therapist would not grant access to the items. A child or adult may also appropriately request the items; again, the therapist would not provide the items. When the child or adult emits the target behavior, aggression, the therapist should immediately and contingently provide access to the tangible items. This allows for teaching of the response–reinforcer relationship. As soon as the individual engages in the response, the therapist provides the reinforcer.

A child or adult may try to grab the tangible items from the therapist. This behavior may change the way in which the condition is carried out. For example, the therapist may have a little cabinet with a key. The therapist could then take the materials away, put them in the cabinet, lock it, and move away. The therapist may pick a high value reinforcer that he or she has better control over. For example, a remote control that starts and stops a preferred video—after the minute presession the therapist can hit pause and put the remote in his or her pocket. The key is that the therapist must have control over terminating the reinforcer. If access to the reinforcer cannot be controlled, the internal validity of your assessment will be compromised because the protocol is not being implemented as intended.

Demand (Sr$^-$)

An escape condition is a test for social negative reinforcement. The presence of the therapist, the work materials, and the instruction, "Let's do some work," serve as discriminative stimuli signaling the availability of escape contingent upon the target behavior. The establishing operation goes into effect with the presentation of moderately difficult demands, which we could consider as being a task in which the child or adult can achieve about 50%–70% accuracy. These types of demands should present enough of a challenge to create an antecedent condition from which the child or adult is motivated to escape. If demands are too aversive, you may observe a high level of emotional responding, which could make it challenging to conduct your session. If demands are easy, the establishing operation (EO) for problem behavior may not be sufficient. Removal of work demands serves as the negative reinforcer.

Conducting the escape condition

The therapist begins the session by making a statement, such as "It's time to do some work" and then presents the task and delivers instruction using least to most prompting (independent, model/gesture, full physical). For example, "Bobby point to purple (independent); point to purple like me (model); let me help you point to purple (full physical)," with 3–5 seconds between prompts. If the child or adult complies with either the verbal or model/gesture prompt, the therapist provides enthusiastic praise, such as "Nice job, that's pointing to purple." If a full physical prompt is needed, the therapist should state what the child or adult did in a neutral tone of voice, such as "That's pointing to purple." There should be a contrast between a full physical prompt statement and the praise associated with the initial instruction and model/gesture prompt to help the child or adult discriminate between the two different statements. If the child or adult engages in the challenging target behavior, the therapist should remove the task and provide 20 seconds of escape.

If a target response occurs during the escape interval, the therapist may reset the escape interval or let the interval elapse, return to instruction, then remove the task materials again after the first instance of the target behavior. It is the therapist's choice about how to proceed, but it is imperative to clearly define the procedures so that everyone running a session is doing it in the same manner. When interpreting results, consideration of how the structure of the session might have influenced the results will be important.

Automatic reinforcement (Sr^+ or Sr^-)

The attention, tangible, and escape conditions are all tests for social reinforcers maintaining challenging behavior. The last condition to be reviewed is the "maybe this has nothing to do with me" condition. This ignore or alone condition is a test for automatic reinforcement—a way to determine if the target behavior is motivated by consequences produced by the behavior itself. Typical examples of behaviors that produce reinforcing consequences by performing them include turning a channel to a music station, motor stereotypy, selecting a preferred video from a website, and dancing.

Consider this example: a boy comes into your program with a history of property destruction. He throws things all over the place, and naturally, when the teachers give him materials for academic instructions, such as laminated cards, he takes these cards and tosses them, and they go flying everywhere. The teacher huffs and puffs, picks up the materials, and brings them back. As soon as the child gets them back, he throws them everywhere. Your immediate thought may be, "This child doesn't want to do his work! His property destruction is escape maintained!"

However, you may want to give this some additional thought. Perhaps spend some time with the child outside of this environment. Perhaps have a team of clinicians spend time with him, monitor his behaviors separately from each other, and then come back to compare notes. Perhaps the boy simply enjoys watching things fly through the air. If this were to be the case, in an alone condition, we could litter the room with learning materials, exit the room to an observation area, and watch what the child does. If he throws the materials around during alone sessions, it may be that this behavior has nothing to do with escape and is instead maintained by automatic reinforcement.

This is something the authors have witnessed—we assessed a child who threw cards that stuck in the ceiling and then he jumped up and tried to get them. He threw the cards behind him, above him, all the while laughing. He just did this for an entire 30 minutes alone session. The behavior persisted in the absence of any signal of availability of social reinforcement. That is the purpose of an alone condition. It helps you determine if the behavior would occur even when no social consequences are available, which provides evidence for an automatic reinforcement function.

Conducting an alone session

When conducting an alone session, there is no person in the room to deliver any social consequences, which eliminates the possible S^D signaled by a therapist's presence. The alone condition reduces the chance that behavior will occur if social reinforcement is responsible for the maintenance of problem behavior. It is important to note that just because a behavior is maintained by automatic reinforcement, this does not exclude the possibility that social reinforcers may also be maintaining variables. A behavior can have multiple functions.

Additional considerations for the ignore condition

Always remember that while you are ignoring behaviors, you still need to monitor safety and make sure that you are not putting a child, adult, or yourself in a dangerous situation. If the individual with whom you are working with has a nontarget behavior of pulling hair, you may add in a safety component such as wearing a swim cap and a hooded sweatshirt. If hair-pulling is the target behavior, you may consider wearing a wig or extensions. You must make sure you are not ignoring such safety concerns. If you are analyzing elopement, make sure that there is an area you can conduct your assessment to minimize the risks associated with elopement (e.g., empty rooms in a locked wing rather than near an exit close to a busy road). It may pose too great of a risk to ignore automatically maintained SIB that is severe (e.g., eye gouging or biting an open wound that is not healing properly). These considerations need to be made of all conditions, not just the ignore condition. For example, in the tangible condition, if you are studying SIB, you may need to consider how you will protect yourself if the child or adult might engage in aggressive behavior.

Overview of the play (control) condition
The final condition to review is the control or play condition. During this condition, the therapist is attempting to eliminate all potential social establishing operations by giving access to attention at a steady pace, access to preferred items, and no demands being presented. In this scenario, there should be little motivation for problem behavior if it is socially maintained. Automatically maintained behavior, such as whistling, or some form of motor stereotypy, may continue to occur regardless of what social reinforcers are provided noncontingently. There should be abolishing operations in effect for social functions for this condition if the reinforcer is social, because there should be no deprivation from positive reinforcers and no presence of aversive antecedent conditions.

Conducting a play session
One way the control/play condition has been setup within the literature is to provide attention on a fixed-time interval, as well as contingent upon demands or requests for attention. The therapist provides attention on a fixed schedule, and then if the child or adult recruits attention, for example, by saying "Oh look at my toy!" the therapist might say, "I like it!" If the child or adult held the toy up in the air, the therapist might remark "What a cool toy!" In this regard, the therapist is not extinguishing appropriate behavior that is likely maintained by attention. Instead, he or she is reinforcing appropriate behavior, while also providing attention on a fixed schedule in case the child or adult is not efficient at requesting attention. There are no programmed consequences for the target response in the play condition, and if the therapist is scheduled to deliver attention based upon the fixed schedule and problem behavior occurs, a 5-second delay should occur prior to providing attention on the fixed schedule.

2.3 Reproducible figures and forms
The figures which have been referenced throughout this chapter are presented below. These can be photocopied for use during training sessions.

CHAPTER 3

Conducting functional analysis sessions with children and adults

3.1 Overview of training procedures

Once trainees have demonstrated that they can conduct standard functional analysis (FA) sessions with a high degree of accuracy, and sessions are conducted with children and adults. Trainers should coordinate with clinicians in their program to determine which individuals may benefit from a standard FA and which behaviors should be assessed.

This component of training is included in the curriculum to promote the generalization of skills and to provide additional practice conducting sessions so that trainees can become more fluent in basic FA procedures. For example, under the supervision of the trainer, trainees now need to speak with caregivers to obtain consent to conduct an FA (see Section 3.3 at the end of this chapter), identify a location for the assessment, and coordinate with other team members to schedule the assessment. In addition, conducting sessions with children and adults often presents many other challenges that are not captured in the simulated conditions. For instance, a child or adult may start to exhibit other nontarget behaviors that are dangerous, or engage in behaviors that make assessment difficult, such as leaving or refusing to enter the assessment room and going to sleep.

We have encountered many of these types of situations in our experience and believe it is beneficial for trainees to be exposed to such challenges under the guidance of the supervising trainer. Trainees also sometimes get the opportunity to observe challenges that are discussed later in the curriculum, such as conducting sessions, during which the target behavior never occurs, the sessions are conducted in the natural setting, and the child or adult gains access to tangibles or attention that were not intended to be part of the assessment.

At the conclusion of this level, trainees will demonstrate the foundational skills to conduct standard FA sessions and, potentially, become more aware of the logistical challenges that need to be taken into consideration when planning an FA. Some organizations may also wish to train a variety of staff, including those providing direct-care services, up to this level, to broaden the number of employees who can perform the function of being a therapist in sessions. Later levels of training may then be reserved for employees who will eventually be asked to design and interpret FAs.

Training steps for Level 2
1. Trainers coordinate with trainee and family of the child or adult to conduct an FA using standard conditions.
2. Trainee conducts sessions and his or her performance is measured using the *Level 2 functional analysis feedback forms* (see Section 3.3 at the end of this chapter).

Criterion to pass Level 2
Score 90% or higher for five conditions during FA sessions with a child or adult (Attention, Escape, Play, Tangible, and Alone or Ignore).

3.2 Practicing standard functional analysis sessions with children and adults

Adapting and selecting standard functional analysis conditions for the assessment

When designing a standard FA, there are many different variables to consider and plan for in advance. It may be the case that not all of the test conditions in Iwata et al. (1982/1994) will be conducted. That is, you may only need or want to test two or three of the functions, as appropriate for the individual situation. There are also considerations in terms of the length of each session, and the particular sequence of sessions that you will be implementing. Materials that will be used in the test condition, such as the work demands, or the type of attention that might be contingent upon the occurrence of the problem behavior, or preferred items for use in the tangible conditions, will need to be individualized to make sure that the proper conditions exist to evoke the target behavior. For example, a child or adult may exhibit aggression when a video stops playing but remains calm when playing a game of catch is terminated.

The typical conditions of an FA include attention, tangible, escape/demands, play, and alone/ignore. Some of the time, not all five conditions need to be involved in the FA. Although trainees will be asked to demonstrate competence for all five conditions, care must be taken to ensure that a child or adult is only exposed to a necessary number of conditions. Through interviewing people familiar with the child or adult, you might learn that one or two of the functions cannot be (or never are) relevant to or influential in the target behavior. Making such determinations will allow a more efficient analysis to be conducted while also providing only those services necessary to help learn more about the person's behavior. Test only those conditions that may be relevant to the particular target behavior under study.

Session duration

A decision has also to be made about the duration of each session. Traditionally, longer sessions have been used, such as 10 or 15 minutes. However, over the years, systematic replications have shown that briefer sessions, such as those 5 minutes in length, can produce valid results as well. Trial-based FAs, which we will discuss later, have even shorter session lengths and can be valid too. One also needs to consider that the goal of the FA is to evoke the target behavior so we can better understand what produces and maintains the behavior so an effective treatment can be developed. Session length can therefore play a role in creating an establishing operation (EO) that is strong enough to evoke behavior.

Determining the sequence of sessions

Usually, sessions are conducted in a random order. The clinician may wish to put sessions in a particular order to take advantage of sequencing effects that can occur. For example, if the clinician suspects an attention function, the EO for attention may be strengthened if an alone session is conducted first, followed by an attention condition; or perhaps running a play condition first could abolish the value of toy play so that the target behavior is less likely to occur in the tangible condition that follows. These are the types of considerations to be made based upon the particular client with whom you are working.

Selection of materials

If you are conducting FA with a child who does not like doing mathematics worksheets, then select those materials for the demand condition. You would not use these materials, however, if you are conducting FA with a child who enjoys mathematics. Attending to these types of details builds our confidence that we are setting up the relevant establishing operations for each test condition.

Determining therapists for the sessions

Once all of the sessions are designed and the materials selected, ask the question, "Who will be playing the role of the therapist in each session?" One therapist could conduct all of the sessions or different therapists could be assigned to each different condition. This decision will be made in part based on available resources and personnel. Using the same therapist for all conditions establishes consistency and reduces the probability of response variability due to therapist differences (e.g., enthusiasm in voice, tactile force of providing physical attention, loudness of voice, nonverbal reactions). However, there are also some advantages if you assign a different therapist for each condition while keeping the same therapist for sessions for each condition. In other words, Therapist A could conduct all attention sessions, Therapist B could conduct all tangible sessions, and Therapist C could conduct all escape sessions. This arrangement may help a child or adult clearly discriminate between the conditions and allow us to detect behavior change that occurs immediately when a new condition starts.

If you were to keep the therapist the same across conditions, differentiation could be achieved in another manner, such as incorporating stimuli unique to each condition. For example, there can be different colored tablecloth-associated attention, escape, and tangible conditions; or the therapist could wear different colored hats or shirts in each condition. These changes help one to signal to the child or adult about what conditions or contingencies are in place for the upcoming session. If successful, we see quicker changes, such as rapid recurrence of the problem behavior or an immediate cessation of the problem behavior, when the discriminative stimuli change.

Obtaining consent

It is imperative to obtain a written consent from the parents or guardians of a child and adult prior to conducting FA. The consent form outlines the reasons, risks, benefits, and procedures associated with FA. Be sure to prepare a consent form in a language that parents and guardians will understand and can be reviewed with them in person. Consent must be obtained for every FA, even if the same behavior is targeted for assessment. The *consent for FA* form in Section 3.3 outlines the conversation that should take place as part of obtaining written consent for an FA.

Supervised implementation of functional analysis sessions

Risk is inherent in FA procedures. Supervision of trainees in FAs is essential and should continue until there is confidence in the trainee's skills. Forms for procedural integrity in each condition can be found in Section 3.3. Consistent adherence to these procedural integrity measures across all conditions should be demonstrated before the trainee is permitted to conduct FAs without on-site trainer support.

Risk prevention guidelines

Implementers of FAs must be continually assessing for and mitigating risk. Trainee competence is one key way to reduce risk, and the trainer should insist upon supervised implementation until proficiency is consistently demonstrated. In addition, medical clearance and oversight are essential. Decisions about health risks should be discussed with medical personnel in an interdisciplinary context before the assessment is conducted. Finally, variations in procedures can be used to minimize risk. These alterations will be reviewed in other levels of the curriculum and should be considered when a traditional FA might pose too many risks.

3.3 Reproducible figures and forms

The figures that have been referenced throughout this chapter are presented later. They can be photocopied for use during training sessions.

Level 2 Functional Analysis Feedback Form – Alone

Date: _____ Trainee: _____ Trainer: _____

Client: _____

Alone Condition

Correct Trainee Response	Present (+) or Absent (-)	Overall Accuracy
Trainee walks into barren room with child or adult participant and states, "Wait here, I'll be back in a few minutes"		
Trainee leaves the room		
Trainee starts timer for session		
Trainee observes child or adult participant for safety (code on Whole Interval – 1')*		
Total Accuracy = $\frac{\text{\# of "+" scores}}{\text{\# of "+" and "-" scores}}$ ⟶		

*At least one instance of the target behavior must occur in order to score this condition

Total Accuracy ≥ 90%?   Yes   No   Cannot Score

Level 2 Functional Analysis Feedback Form – Escape

Date: _____ Trainee: _____ Trainer: _____

Client: _____

Escape Condition

Correct Trainee Response	Present (+) or Absent (-)	Overall Accuracy
Trainee starts timer for session		
Trainee presents child or adult participant with moderately challenging task at a continuous pace		
Trainee praises correct responses to vocal or gesture prompts (score first 10 instances)*		
Trainee makes neutral statement if full physical prompt is needed for accurate response ("that's purple")*		
Trainee removes task and turns away from client contingent upon target behavior*		
Non-target behaviors ignored*		
Trainee presents task again following 20" absence of target behavior*		
Total Accuracy = $\frac{\text{\# of "+" scores}}{\text{\# of "+" and "-" scores}}$ ⟶		

*At least one instance of the target behavior must occur in order to score this condition

Total Accuracy ≥ 90%?   Yes   No   Cannot Score

Conducting functional analysis sessions with children and adults 33

Level 2 Functional Analysis Feedback Form – Play

Date: _____ Trainee: _____ Trainer: _____
Client: _____

Play (FT 20" + DRA)			
Correct Trainee Response	Present (+) or Absent (-)		Overall Accuracy
Trainee starts timer for session			
Trainee presents child or adult participant with 2-3 highly preferred toys and states "here are some toys to play with"			
Trainee is oriented to client, remains within 3 ft throughout the session			
Trainee provides vocal and physical attention every 20" (score first 10 opportunities) *			
Trainee institutes a delay of 5" if the target behavior occurs when attention is to be provided*			
Trainee ignores target behavior*			
Trainee responds to appropriate requests or intraverbals related to attention ("Check out my car) *			
Total Accuracy = $\frac{\text{\# of "+" scores}}{\text{\# of "+" and "-" scores}}$ ⟶			

*At least one instance of the target behavior must occur in order to score this condition

Total Accuracy ≥ 90%?   Yes   No   Cannot Score

Functional Analysis

Level 2 Functional Analysis Feedback Form – Attention

Date: _____ Trainee: _____ Trainer: _____

Client: _____

Attention Condition		
Correct Staff Response	Present (+) or Absent (-)	Overall Accuracy
Child-adult and therapist are in a room with moderately preferred items		
Therapist starts timer for the session		
Therapist states, "I have some work to do," picks up a book, and moves a minimum of 5 feet away from the client		
Therapist delivers 3-5 s of attention (physical and verbal attention) contingent upon target behavior (per first 10 occurrence)		
Walks a minimum of 5 feet away and attends to reading material after attention is provided (per occurrence)		
Non-target behaviors ignored (per occurrence)		
Total Accuracy = $\frac{\text{\# of "+" scores}}{\text{\# of "+" and "-" scores}}$ $\longrightarrow$		

*At least one instance of the target behavior must occur in order to score this condition

Total Accuracy ≥ 90%?   Yes   No   Cannot Score

Level 2 Functional Analysis Feedback Form – Tangible

Date: _____ Trainee: _____ Trainer: _____
Client: _____

Tangible		
Correct Trainee Response	Present (+) or Absent (-)	Overall Accuracy
Trainee presents child-adult with highly preferred materials for 1 min prior to session		
Trainee ignores all pre-session behaviors (appropriate and inappropriate)		
Trainee starts timer and takes away materials at start of session		
Trainee returns materials for 20" contingent upon target behavior (score first 10 instances)*		
Trainee takes materials away after child-adult has not engaged in the target behavior for 20" (score first 10 instances)*		
Trainee ignores non-target behavior		
Total Accuracy = $\dfrac{\text{\# of "+" scores}}{\text{\# of "+" and "-" scores}}$ ⟶		

*At least one instance of the target behavior must occur in order to score this condition

Total Accuracy ≥ 90%?   Yes   No   Cannot Score

Level 2 Functional Analysis Feedback Form – Ignore

Date: _____ Trainee: _____ Trainer: _____

Client: _____

Ignore Condition		
Correct Trainee Response	Present (+) or Absent (-)	Overall Accuracy
Trainee starts timer for session		
Trainee observes child-adult for safety (code on Whole Interval – 1')*		
Trainee ignores each instance of the target behavior*		
Trainee ignores all non-target behavior throughout the session		
Total Accuracy = $\dfrac{\text{\# of ``+'' scores}}{\text{\# of ``+'' and ``-'' scores}}$ →		

*At least one instance of the target behavior must occur in order to score this condition

Total Accuracy ≥ 90%?   Yes   No   Cannot Score

Consent for functional analysis

Proper treatment relies on knowing the events that influence an individual's behavior. A number of data collection tools may be used to obtain these data. Such tools have been shown to be effective in clinical practice. One method that is often needed to identify why an individual is engaging in challenging behavior is an FA. When doing an FA, it is necessary to collect precise data to assist in developing a behavior intervention plan.

Why do we do functional analysis?

The reason for doing FAs is that we need more data about when, where, and why challenging behaviors occur to write treatment plans. At times, prior assessment (such as a descriptive analysis, in which data are collected in the natural environment) has yielded inadequate information to guide treatment. We may not have obtained enough information to make us confident of analyzing why this individual is experiencing this behavior. An FA can assist us in clarifying the nature of the problem and the context(s) in which the behavior occurs. This helps us more certainly know the purpose (or function) of the challenging behavior. When treatment is matched to the function (the reason it occurs) of the challenging behavior, we see better outcomes. Without an FA to guide us, target behaviors may increase, delaying the implementation of an effective strategy and potentially posing a safety risk to the individual we are serving. FAs increase the precision and efficiency of assessing and treating severe and complex behavioral challenges and lead to more effective interventions.

How do we do functional analysis?
The main method we use to conduct FAs is to systematically create contexts to see if the target behavior occurs at different rates. We are interested in seeing what types of conditions and consequences result in low rates of the problem behavior, and which conditions and consequences lead to higher rates. For example, clinicians may present tasks that are nonpreferred and may remove those tasks once the challenging behavior occurs. Alternatively, we may reduce our interaction with the individual and give attention only when the target behavior occurs. With this kind of precision and data analysis, we can make the best decisions about how to treat the behavior.

Who do functional analyses do?
FAs are a team effort. FAs also require the selection of experienced staff with supervised experience in conducting FAs to guide and supervise the process. A multitier training process is used to ensure that the individuals involved in FAs have demonstrated their competence. If a child or adult client engages in severe problem behavior that poses a safety risk, we have particular types of FAs we can use to minimize risks, such as analyzing a milder form of the behavior that predicts the more severe form (e.g., a client slapping the table often leads to self-injury). In addition, if we believe, there is a risk that the client participating in the FA may exhibit dangerous behavior, we may ensure medical oversight throughout the process.

By signing below, I consent that:

I have been informed of the basis and merits of FAs.

I have had the chance to discuss the way the FA will be conducted.

I know that one of the goals of a FA is to determine what leads to the onset and maintenance of my dependent's problem behavior by systematically arranging conditions and consequences that were identified during prior assessments, such as interviews and observations.

I know I have a right to request or view literature on the use of FAs.

I know that if my dependent engages in dangerous behavior, nursing/medical staff (on-site or on-call) will be notified when an FA is going to be conducted so they can be available if any needed medical support is necessary.

I know that the goal is to maintain the safety and welfare of the individual participating in the FA, and that there are types of FAs that can be used to minimize risk of injury or stress.

I know that I will see the data from the FA when it is completed.

I understand that I can revoke my consent at any time by writing to _____. I can also request for it to be modified to meet my approval. I do however understand that my refusal to sign or changes to the consent may be in conflict with program goals, thereby necessitating a meeting with agency personnel.

This consent will be re-distributed for review and approval on an annual basis or whenever a new FA is deemed to be warranted. This consent (for this behavior) remains valid until the annual renewal is completed. If there are any changes to the consent, a new consent will be distributed. Any new FA (including on this behavior within the year) will require additional written consent.

_____   _____
Parent/Guardian Signature   Date

_____   _____
Clinician/Administrator Signature   Date

CHAPTER 4

Extending standard functional analysis conditions

4.1 Overview of training procedures

During the third level of the curriculum, trainees are introduced to various modifications to the standard conditions that have been described in the literature, such as the divided attention condition (Fahmie, Iwata, Harper, & Querim, 2013; Mace, Page, Ivancic, & O'Brien, 1986; Taylor, Sisson, McKelvey, & Trefelner, 1993), and the evaluation of different types of attention that may serve as a reinforcer (Kodak, Northup, & Kelley, 2007; Piazza et al., 1999). In addition, novel conditions that have been developed and are commonly used are also discussed, such as social avoidance condition (Harper, Iwata, & Camp, 2013). Evaluating the potential for multiple functions is also reviewed (e.g., Moore, Mueller, Dubard, Roberts, & Sterling-Turner, 2002; Mueller, Sterling-Turner, & Moore, 2005).

Similar to other training levels, we reviewed the literature and then created training materials to represent these modified and novel conditions rather than handing out articles for trainees to read. Because there is variation in how each of these different conditions is conducted across articles, we believed it might be confusing for our trainees. The trainer may wish, however, to distribute a list of references for trainees who are interested.

After reviewing conditions created by other professionals in the field of behavior analysis, we then teach trainees how they can create their own conditions based upon the idiosyncrasies of the children and adults that they serve and the environments in which problem behavior is observed through open-ended interviews and descriptive analyses to inform the development of unique and experimentally sound test and control conditions (Hanley, 2012).

Training steps for Level 3
1. Trainer conducts slideshow presentation

2. Trainee takes *extending standard functional analysis (FA) conditions quiz* (Fig. 4.1)
3. Quizzes are scored using the *extending standard FA conditions quiz answer key* (Fig. 4.2)

Criteria to pass Level 3
- Score of 90% or higher on *extending standard FA conditions quiz*

4.2 Developing unique functional analysis conditions

The first two levels reviewed the basics about how to conduct a standard FA (Iwata et al., 1982/1994). Notably, the efficacy of the standard FA has been replicated numerous times within the literature (Beavers, Iwata, & Lerman, 2013; Hanley, Iwata, & McCord, 2003). However, over time, clinicians and researchers have continued to explore how variations in antecedents and consequences influence levels of challenging behavior during the FA. The method described by Iwata et al. (1982/1994) provided a structure or assessment format on which others could expand to additional conditions.

A number of variations to the standard FA conditions have been published in the literature such as the divided attention condition (Fahmie, Iwata, Harper, et al., 2013; Fahmie, Iwata, Querim, & Harper, 2013) and social avoidance condition (Harper et al., 2013). In this section, we will discuss published extensions of the standard FA conditions as well as the steps to create unique test-control conditions with children and adults.

Divided attention
As described by Fahmie et al., this condition is conducted in the same manner as the attention condition, except, at the start of the session, the therapist states, "Here are some toys to play with; I am going to talk to someone else." The antecedent is talking to another peer or dividing your attention between the child–adult and someone else. The consequence for the challenging behavior is the termination of the therapist's attention to another person followed by vocal and physical attention to the child or adult. Keep in mind that there are technically two consequences for the challenging behavior in this condition—the termination of talking between therapists (which could be a negative

reinforcement contingency) and the delivery of attention (possible positive reinforcement contingency).

Variations of attention
The way in which attention is delivered may affect levels of behavior during the assessment. For example, you could provide physical touch or deliver verbal attention in isolation. The point here is that not all types of attention will affect behavior in the same way. The functional reinforcer for challenging behavior may consist of attention in the form of verbal reprimands. In this case, statements of concern may not produce elevated rates of behavior.

Variations of escape
During the test condition for negative reinforcement in the standard FA, task demands are presented as the potential aversive event. However, recall that aversive events are idiosyncratic and thus may vary from individual to individual. For example, dancing may be aversive, or something avoided, to an individual who does not have rhythm, but it may not be considered an aversive event to someone who knows how to dance. Several examples of how to incorporate different general categories of potential aversive events have been demonstrated within the FA literature. For example, research has been published examining escape from medical procedures, noise, different types of demands, and social avoidance.

Iwata et al. (1990) described a modified demand condition based upon observations that a child or adult tended to engage in SIB when undergoing medical examination. The condition was arranged so that questions related to medical examination (e.g., "Does your knee hurt, can you move it for me?") served as the antecedent condition and the therapist (emulating a medical professional) ceased asking questions and turned away contingent upon self-injurious behavior (SIB).

McCord et al. (2001) described a procedure for selecting aversive noises to include in an FA based upon information obtained during interviews. During the FA, these noises (e.g., alarm clock, phone ringing, person talking) were played at the start of the session and then terminated for 30 seconds following challenging behavior.

Roscoe et al. (2009) described a demands assessment in which different activities to be included in an FA were selected based upon interview results. A variety of tasks were identified across different domains (academics, daily living skills, and domestic skills) and designated as either high-or low-probability tasks in relation to the degree of compliance observed in the demands assessment. During the FA, either one high-probability or two low-probability demands were presented and then demands were terminated for 30 seconds contingency upon challenging behavior.

Social avoidance is another type of escape (Harper et al., 2013). An example would be when a therapist and child are in a room with moderately preferred items (2–3 toys). The therapist provides attention in the form of statements, with a physical contact for every 5 s. This will look very much like the play condition where you are delivering frequent attention. Once the challenging behavior occurs, the therapist turns and moves away. The contingency here is challenging behavior that results in the removal of social interaction.

Screening for automatic reinforcement

As we discussed in previous trainings, in the ignore condition, you can use a one-way mirror, camera, sunglasses (to avoid eye contact), or hands behind your back to increase the saliency of the contingency, or lack of social contingencies. It is important to remain neutral and not provide any possible form of attention (e.g., facial expressions, eye contact) when conducting the ignore condition. The previous research has suggested that an extended alone or ignore condition can be conducted following an FA with undifferentiated results to provide evidence for an automatic function (Vollmer et al., 1995). Querim et al. (2013) extended this research to suggest that one might conduct the extended alone/ignore conditions prior to, or maybe even in replacement of, the standard FA if the hypothesis is that the challenging behavior is maintained by automatic reinforcement.

Variations to the control session

There are slight variations in the way the control, or play condition is conducted across studies. However, there is limited published research comparing such variations. One study conducted by Fahmie, Iwata, Harper, et al. (2013) and Fahmie, Iwata, Querim, et al. (2013) concluded that the alone, ignore, play, and differential reinforcement of other behavior (DRO) conditions served as effective control conditions for challenging behavior maintained by positive reinforcement, but the

DRO condition was not an effective control condition when evaluating challenging behavior maintained by negative reinforcement. No matter what variation of the control condition one chooses to include, the critical component is that the only difference between the two conditions is the contingency, which is the most experimentally sound comparison you could make.

Multiple functions

In some cases, challenging behavior is said to be multiply maintained. Such a statement could reference a few different scenarios. We will discuss two potential ways in which the behavior of a child or adult might be maintained by multiple contingencies. We are using the term "multiple functions" to describe situations during which challenging behavior is maintained by a single reinforcer in one setting (e.g., tangible), but a different reinforcer (e.g., attention) in another setting, as well as when challenging behavior is maintained by more than one reinforcer simultaneously (e.g., escape and attention) in the same setting. Let us take a moment to discuss this in a bit more detail.

Different contexts/consequences

It is possible that multiple functions are present when the same behavior is maintained by different consequences under different circumstances. For example, a child or adult may engage in aggression in the presence of a teacher delivering instruction because it typically results in removal of task demands, but aggression may also occur in front of a parent because it typically results in the parent asking what is wrong and providing tangible items as a distractor. This type of multiple function would likely be identified by a standard FA.

Paired consequences

In some cases, challenging behavior is maintained by a set of paired consequences. For example, a student may sweep work materials off of the desk because this typically results in escape from work and a frustrated reaction (attention) by the teacher. If both of these consequences are necessary to maintain this disruptive behavior, then we would say the behavior is multiply maintained by the paired consequences. Although the standard FA may identify such multiple functions, at times, it may be necessary to combine antecedent or consequent events to evoke the challenging behavior during the assessment.

Developing unique test and control conditions

We are going to switch gears a bit and discuss the process of creating unique test-control conditions when trying to identify the function of challenging behavior. Much of what we will cover in this section really applies to all functional behavior assessments (FBAs).

When planning your FA during the interview and observation process, you may identify idiosyncratic variables that either evoke or maintain challenging behavior. The key to understanding what motivates behavior includes the following:

1. Figuring out what is going to evoke a behavior (what antecedent conditions, or establishing operations)
2. Determining what consequences maintain that challenging behavior (reinforcers)

In order to figure out what the relevant variables are, interview caregivers who spend time with the child or adult and observe the child or adult when the potential establishing operation (EO)/consequences are operating. Be sure to interview those who have recently or currently spent a lot of time with the child or adult. Remember, we are not trying to identify what first established the behavior; rather we are trying to identify what is currently maintaining the behavior. Therefore caregiver involvement will vary depending on how involved the caregivers are at the time of assessment.

Questions that uncover EOs/consequences

Ask questions about what types of events precede challenging behavior because these are the conditions you may build into your test condition in an FA. Some questions you can ask are "What kind of activities are happening right before challenging behavior occurs? What seems to trigger challenging behavior? When do you see the behavior the most? Can you predict when your child's challenging behavior will occur?" This last question may also help you identify precursor behaviors. If the behavior you are considering evaluating has a high risk of harm associated with it, you may want to consider a precursor FA during which you evaluate a different challenging behavior that typically precedes the more dangerous one.

Next, you want to ask about the consequences. How do people typically respond to the challenging behavior? How can you help the child or adult settle down once he or she is upset? Understanding the answers to these types of questions can help you determine how to respond in your test condition but also determine what elements to build into the antecedent condition of your control condition. For example, a caregiver may indicate that when on the phone, the child or adult typically engages in SIB. In response, the caregiver approaches the child or adult to see what he needs and finds an object that typically settles him. In this case, you may want to evaluate for a possible tangible function. In your test condition, you would provide an object contingent upon the challenging behavior, and in the control condition, you would provide the object noncontingently, prior to the onset of challenging behavior.

These are the types of things to identify during an interview and observation. You can also adjust potentially relevant variables when you are observing, such as asking a teacher to talk with you for a few minutes to see if deprivation from attention may be relevant. Alternatively, you might ask a teacher to deliver a certain type of instructional task you think might evoke escape-maintained challenging behavior.

Creating conditions

There are multiple ways you can develop test and control conditions, and each has its own strengths and limitations. We are going to tell you about our preferred methodology. However, there are no explicit rules. You can design conditions in any manner you like, as long as your design is experimentally sound. We have recommended certain ways to design negative-reinforcement contingencies and positive-reinforcement contingencies, because of the side effects associated with different approaches.

When creating a test condition, your antecedent condition should include an S^D to signal availability of a particular consequence. The EO should be present to increase the value of the consequence and therefore the frequency of the behavior. When the target behavior occurs, it should result in immediate, brief access to the consequence(s) hypothesized to be maintaining the behavior. These consequences should only be provided following the target behavior.

In contrast to the test condition, the EO should be absent during the control condition to minimize the probability that the challenging behavior will occur. In this regard, the consequences utilized in the test condition are instead presented noncontingently in the control condition. A common control condition for behavior maintained by positive reinforcement, such as the contingent delivery of attention or tangibles, is noncontingent reinforcement (NCR). If free access is allowed, there should be no deprivation in effect. You should observe no challenging behavior if that is the functional reinforcer.

In the test condition, you are attempting to create a state of deprivation by removing the toys/attention and withholding them until the challenging behavior occurs. This establishes the contingency, which should then motivate the individual to engage in challenging behavior. A major advantage of using NCR in your control condition is that it is very practical. You just give attention, toys, or some other form of leisure throughout the session. It is a very easy way to conduct a control condition. It also isolates the contingency as the sole difference between the test and control conditions, because the putative reinforcer is present in both conditions. The only difference is that in one, it is presented for free and in the other, it is delivered contingent upon the target behavior of study. By isolating the contingency as the sole difference between the control and test conditions, you establish strong internal validity for your assessment.

Control condition for negative-reinforcement contingency

The control condition for negative reinforcement is much different. When evaluating the impact of negative reinforcers, we recommend a methodology of EO present versus EO absent. In your test condition, the negative reinforcer is presented at the start of the session and then is removed contingent upon the challenging behavior. The EO is present in your test condition because you are delivering, for example, a work task. The delivery of work is the evocative event. You are delivering it and then, contingent upon challenging behavior, you are removing the demands. In the control condition, the stimuli are never presented, so the EO is absent (if, of course, this variable is relevant to motivating the child or adult to perform the target behavior). Because the negative reinforcer is an aversive event, we do not want to present it at all, as it may evoke challenging behavior, and our goal in control conditions is to suppress the occurrence of the challenging behavior.

True noncontingent negative reinforcement would involve presenting work, and removing it noncontingently on a scheduled basis. However, presenting work may evoke challenging behavior and may make it difficult for the child or adult to discriminate between your test and control conditions because you are approaching with work in each condition. A problem with not introducing work is that you have changed two things between the conditions. You have a contingency in one and not in the other, and you have the negative reinforcer in one condition, but not in the other. Therefore you have changed two things, but we are willing to accept that limitation because of the risks of using the aversive stimuli in a control condition. The reader is invited to review the case examples in the accompanying slideshow for this level to see how unique test and control conditions can be designed.

4.3 Reproducible figures and forms

The figures for this section include the quiz used to measure knowledge competency around extending FA conditions, along with the answer key. These figures can be photocopied for use during training sessions.

Name: _____ Date: _____

1. What are the two major differences between the attention and the divided attention condition (2 pts)?

2. What is the antecedent event during the social avoidance condition (1 pt)?

3. What is one advantage to using a DRO contingency during the play condition (1 pt)?

4. Provide an example of a behavior with multiple functions within different contexts not used in the PPT (1 pt).

5. What should you do prior to conducting a test-control functional analysis (1 pt)?

Figure 4.1 Extending functional analysis (FA) conditions quiz.

48 Functional Analysis

6. Describe the general procedures for test and control conditions for behavior maintained by positive reinforcement in the form of attention and behavior maintained negative reinforcement maintained by escape from task demands (2 pts).

Attention Test:

Attention Control:

Escape Test:

Escape Control:

7. Your brother's dog, Sparky, is engaging in whining behavior. You interview your brother and sister-in-law who both report that Sparky usually whines when the family is sitting down for dinner around 5pm and that Sparky eats dinner at 7pm. **Sparky has never accessed food when the family is eating**. When Sparky whines, your brother reprimands him and prompts him to, "go lay on your bed". Sparky typically complies with this prompt but returns to the table and whines within 1 min. What is your hypothesized function of Sparky's whining behavior? Design your test and control conditions for this hypothesis (4 pts).

8. Why would you ask the following question when conducting an interview in preparation for designing a test-control FA: If I was going to give you a million dollars to make the behavior occur, what would you do (1 pt)?

Figure 4.1 (Continued)

9. Why would you ask the following question when conducting an interview in preparation for designing a test-control FA: Is there anything you do that seems to make the behavior go away (1 pt)?

10. Following your interviews and observations, you hypothesize that when a peer screams, your student screams, regardless of the observable consequences that follow your student's screaming. If this were to be the case, what would you hypothesize as the function of your student's screaming? What is the establishing operation? Describe a test condition and a control condition (4 pts).

11. Following your interviews and observations, you hypothesize that your student's food stealing behavior tends to occur around food items. However, you have observed that even when the student acquires food items, he does not attempt to eat them; rather he just holds onto the items. Since staff members quickly intervene physically (blocking) and verbally (e.g., "If you want the chips you can ask for them") after an attempt to steal food, this behavior may be maintained by the combination of verbal and physical attention. If this were to be the case, what would you hypothesize as the function of your student's food stealing behavior? What is the establishing operation? Describe a test condition and a control condition (4 pts).

Figure 4.1 Continued

12. Barry often engages in aggression when his favorite toys are out of reach. When Barry engages in aggression, his caregivers tend to give him the preferred toys to try to settle him down, and this usually works (he exhibits less aggression). What do you hypothesize the function of your student's aggression is? What is the establishing operation? Describe a test condition and a control condition (4 pts).

13. Samantha starts engaging in SIB whenever a staff member brings over a matching task. She used to complete the task each day, but now it is difficult for the staff members to conduct this task because Samantha's SIB is so intense they cannot gain compliance. What do you hypothesize the function of your Samantha's SIB is? What is the establishing operation? Describe a test condition and a control condition (4 pts).

Total Points (out of 30): _____

Figure 4.1 Continued

Extending standard functional analysis conditions 51

1. What are the two major differences between the attention and the divided attention condition (2 pts)?

    1) The antecedent for the divided attention condition involves two therapists talking to each other whereas the attention condition antecedent involves the therapists silently reading.

    2) In the divided attention condition, the therapists cease their conversation, whereas in the attention condition no conversation is occurring.

2. What is the antecedent event during the social avoidance condition (1pt)?

    The therapist delivers continuous attention to the child or adult, remaining within 3 feet of the child or adult until problem behavior occurs.

3. What is one advantage to using a DRO contingency during the play condition (1pt)?

    1) Because the DRO interval resets each time problem behavior occurs, there is no opportunity for adventitious reinforcement.

    OR

    2) Using this procedure as a control allows for a true reversal contingency, which helps to establish better experimental control

4. Provide an example of a behavior with multiple functions within different contexts not used in the PPT (1pt).

    A child's aggression is maintained by escape from demands when a teacher presents a non-preferred task. Aggression is maintained by attention in the home setting during states of low attention.

    Any answer that describes a behavior maintained by a particular consequence in one setting, or with one person, that is also maintained by a different consequence in a different setting or with a different person.

Figure 4.2 Answer key for extending functional analysis (FA) conditions.

5. What should you do prior to conducting a test-control functional analysis (1pt)?

   Interview individuals who know the child or adult well and observe the child or adult to develop a hypothesis about possible functions and determine what to include in your functional analysis.

6. Describe the general procedures for test and control conditions for behavior maintained by positive reinforcement in the form of attention and behavior maintained by negative reinforcement maintained by escape from task demands (2pts).

   For behavior maintained by positive reinforcement:

   Test: Withhold attention as an antecedent condition. Provide access to attention contingent upon problem behavior.

   Control: Provide non-contingent access to attention.

   For behavior maintained by negative reinforcement:

   Test: Present the aversive stimulus (establishing operation present) as the antecedent condition. Remove the aversive stimulus contingent upon problem behavior

   Control: The establishing operation (aversive stimulus) is never presented.

7. Your brother's dog, Sparky, is engaging in whining behavior. You interview your brother and sister-in-law who both report that Sparky usually whines when the family is sitting down for dinner around 5pm and that Sparky eats dinner at 7pm. **Sparky has never accessed food when the family is eating**. When Sparky whines, your brother reprimands him and prompts him to, "go lay on your bed". Sparky typically complies with this prompt but returns to the table and whines within 1 minute. What is your hypothesized function of Sparky's whining behavior? Design your test and control conditions for this hypothesis (4pts).

    a. Hypothesized Function: Attention
    b. EO: Deprivation from attention
    c. Test: In the presence of a meal, provide attention contingent upon whining in the typical reprimand form
    d. Control: Provide continuous attention in the form of reprimands to Sparky in the presence of a meal.

Figure 4.2 Continued

8. Why would you ask the following question when conducting an interview in preparation for designing a test-control FA: If I was going to give you a million dollars to make the behavior occur, what would you do (1pt)?

   To try to determine what antecedent conditions evoke behavior.

9. Why would you ask the following question when conducting an interview in preparation for designing a test-control FA: Is there anything you do that seems to make the behavior go away (1pt)?

   To try to determine what consequences are maintaining problem behavior.

10. Following your interviews and observations, you hypothesize that when a peer screams, your student screams, regardless of the observable consequences that follow your student's screaming. If this were to be the case, what would you hypothesize as the function of your student's screaming? What is the establishing operation? Describe a test condition and a control condition (4pts).

    a. Hypothesized function: Automatic negative reinforcement (if the peer's screaming is aversive) or automatic positive reinforcement (if the peer's screaming is pleasant)
    b. EO: Peer screaming
    c. Test: Present a recording of peer screaming in an alone session; no consequences are provided for the challenging behavior or any other challenging/appropriate behavior
    d. Control: Conduct an alone session with no audio recording; no consequences are provided for the challenging behavior or any other challenging/appropriate behavior

11. Following your interviews and observations, you hypothesize that food stealing behavior tends to occur around food items. However, you have observed that even when the child or adult acquires food items, he does not attempt to eat them; rather he just holds onto the items. Because staff members quickly intervene physically (blocking) and verbally (e.g., "If you want the chips you can ask for them") after an attempt to steal food, this behavior may be maintained by the combination of verbal and physical attention. If this were to be the case, what would you hypothesize for the function of your student's food stealing behavior? What is the establishing operation? Describe a test condition and a control condition (4pts).

Figure 4.2 Continued

a. *Hypothesized function:* Attention in the form of verbal and physical attention
b. *EO:* Deprivation from attention
c. *Test:* In the presence of food items, only provide attention contingent upon an attempt to food steal
d. *Control:* In the presence of food items, provide non-contingent physical and verbal attention

12. Barry often engages in aggression when his favorite toys are out of reach. When Barry engages in aggression, his caregivers tend to give him the preferred toys to try to settle him down, and this usually works (he exhibits less aggression). What do you hypothesize the function of your student's aggression is? What is the establishing operation? Describe a test condition and a control condition (4pts).

    a. *Hypothesized function:* Access to tangible items (preferred toys)
    b. *EO:* Deprivation from tangibles
    c. *Test:* Provide Barry with toys during a 1 min pre-session; remove the toys at the start of the test session and provide 20-30 seconds of access to the toys contingent upon aggression. After 20-30 seconds of access, remove the toys, and provide further access contingent upon aggression.
    d. *Control:* Allow Barry to have noncontingent access to his preferred toys. Do not provide any consequences for appropriate or inappropriate behavior.

13. Samantha starts engaging in SIB whenever a staff member brings over a matching task. She used to complete the task each day, but now it is difficult for the staff members to conduct this task because Samantha's SIB is so intense they cannot gain compliance. What do you hypothesize the function of your Samantha's SIB is? What is the establishing operation? Describe a test condition and a control condition (4pts).

    a. *Hypothesized function:* Escape from academic demands (in particular, the matching task)
    b. *EO:* Presentation of matching task
    c. *Test:* Present the matching task using 3-step prompting. Praise independent correct responses and correct responses following a gesture prompt. Make a neutral statement if full physical prompting is needed. Remove the task for 20 sec and turn away from the child or adult contingent upon SIB. Re-present the task after 20 sec and remove the task again contingent upon SIB.
    d. *Control:* Remain in proximity to the child or adult – do not present the matching task. Do not provide consequences for appropriate or inappropriate behavior.

Total Points = 30 points

Figure 4.2 Continued

CHAPTER 5

Measurement, experimental design, methodology

5.1 Overview of training procedures

The fourth level of this curriculum addresses three central components that need to be considered when designing a functional analysis (FA): selecting an appropriate measurement system for the behavior being assessed, choosing an experimental design which will be used to identify the function of behavior, and selecting the method in which sessions will be structured. This level is of great importance, because it influences how long the assessment will take, addresses potential risks to the child or adult FA participant, and establishes the internal validity of the assessment when identifying a function or functions of behavior.

The measurement component of the curriculum discusses the various continuous recording methods used in behavior analysis along with commonly used discontinuous measurement systems. A variety of resources were used to generate the content for this component of training, including but not limited to, the textbook by Cooper, Heron, and Heward (2007) and articles evaluating critical elements when measuring behavior such as consideration of whether to use one or more target behaviors in an FA (Beavers & Iwata, 2011) and limitations of using discontinuous measurement systems in comparison to continuous recording methods (Meany-Daboul, Roscoe, Bourett, & Ahearn, 2007; Rapp, Carroll, Strangeland, Swanson, & Higgins, 2011).

Common experimental designs are reviewed with content being derived from a variety of textbooks, such as Cooper et al. (2007) and Barlow, Nock, and Hersen (2009). Issues in experimental design specific to FA are also included, based on publications describing how to isolate variables in multielement test−control analyses (e.g., Hanley, Jin, Vanselow, & Hanratty, 2014).

Our methodology component of this curriculum describes the format of the standard FA developed by Iwata et al. (1982/1994) and the many methodological variations that have been described in the literature, such as precursor and trial-based FAs (Hanley et al., 2003; Iwata & Dozier, 2008; Lydon, Healy, O'Reilly, & Lang, 2012). The goal of this review is to prepare the clinician to select and implement the procedure best matched to the presenting behavior, given all logistical, safety, and clinical contextual factors.

Following this level of the curriculum, trainees will have acquired foundational skills for designing and implementing FAs. The next stage of the curriculum then teaches trainees how to graph and interpret the data obtained during these assessments.

Training steps for Level 4
1. Trainer conducts slideshow presentation.
2. Trainee takes the *measurement, experimental design, and methodology quiz* (Fig. 5.1).
3. Quizzes are scored using the *answer key for measurement, experimental design, and methodology quiz* (Fig. 5.2).

Criterion to pass Level 4
- Score of 90% or higher on measurement, experimental design, and methodology quiz

5.2 Measurement
Selecting the target behavior
When selecting a behavior to measure, it is best to make the condition consequences contingent upon a single problem behavior rather than combining behaviors (Beavers et al., 2013). For example, you might have a child or adult who engages in aggression and self-injurious behavior (SIB), and you are not sure which behavior to provide the consequences for because loud noises or work demands could evoke both topographies. If that is the case, just pick one of them. Using multiple target behaviors tends to lead to undifferentiated data and undifferentiated analysis. If you think multiple challenging behaviors are in the same response class, pick the behavior that typically occurs first. You could also provide the session therapist with the definition for two relevant challenging behaviors, such as aggression and SIB, and present the antecedent condition for the session. Upon the first instance of either of these behaviors, the

therapist could provide the consequences and then use that behavior as the target behavior going forward. If the behaviors are in the same response class and you do not provide the reinforcer for one of the challenging behaviors, the child or adult should start to allocate toward the other behavior.

You will also want to take notes about other challenging and appropriate behaviors. If you choose to measure and graph multiple behaviors, make sure you clearly label your graph as to which behavior was contingently reinforced. The other behaviors are tracked just as a way of recognizing that they arose during the FA, and referencing them in your graph may help you to refine your analysis further as you continue to collect data. The audience should be aware, however, of the particular behavior being the target behavior subject to the contingencies of your FA. In terms of a measurement system, continuous recording will always give you the best representation of what is happening in a session, because it is real-time recording that captures every instance of behavior.

Frequency

Frequency of responses during a session is best for responses that are easily countable and have a discrete beginning and end. You also want to select responses that have an interresponse time that is at least 1–2 seconds. If your interresponse times are very quick (e.g., a child or adult may clear surfaces with his hand quickly), accurate counting may be difficult. You should also identify when a behavior begins and ends. For example, if you are measuring rocking behavior, define one instance of rocking as beginning when the child or adult leans forward and ending after the child or adult leans backwards.

Duration

Duration, in contrast, is a reasonable measure for behaviors that last a long time (e.g., crying episodes, dropping, out-of-seat behavior), because frequency is not going to yield much information (i.e., the variability of the data will be very restricted). When recording behaviors by duration, you usually need to start and stop a timing device to accurately record variable episodes. Session data can be converted to a cumulative duration measure or average duration per behavior episode.

Latency

Latency is defined as the time from the end of a discriminative stimulus (cue) to the beginning of a first response and is a good representation of response strength. Latency as a measurement system can be used in various FA methodologies and is efficient because it requires minimal effort to record, and you can also layer the data on to other measures. For example, you may wish to graph the frequency of a challenging behavior while also having a graph depicting latency to first response.

Discontinuous measurement systems

Sometimes we want to measure behaviors that do not have clear start and stop times or behaviors that occur for long durations followed by short durations. The behavior may also have long interresponse times and then short interresponse times. In this case, you may want to consider partial interval recording (PIR) or momentary time sampling (MTS). These discontinuous measurement systems are reported as percent intervals, but you should also indicate that you are either estimating frequency, duration, or both. In addition, you should translate these data for your audience, so they are aware of the approximate frequency and/or duration you are estimating.

Calculating estimated frequency and duration

For MTS, you define a specific window so that two observers will record behavior consistently. In a 10-second interval, you identify the exact moment during which you are looking for that behavior. In this example, it could be the 1-second interval at the end of the 10-second segment (9.00–9.99 seconds). It would be the momentary time window that you code. With PIR the person collecting data records whether or not the behavior occurred at any point during the predefined interval window. In this example the data collector would code a " + " if the behavior occurred at any point during 0.00–9.99 seconds, and a " − " if it did not.

MTS is generally a more accurate measurement system than PIR, although Rapp, Colby-Dirksen, Michalski, Carroll, and Lindenberg (2008) demonstrated how these systems compare across varying interval windows and the dimension of behavior that is estimated. When selecting an interval recording measurement system, choosing a shorter interval duration, such as 5 seconds, will minimize estimation error.

When the interval becomes longer, such as 10, 20 seconds, or higher, PIR may inaccurately represent overall occurrence of behavior. MTS does a better job at estimating behavior, but it also has poor correspondence with actual rates of behavior when the interval is set at higher durations. If you use one of these discontinuous methods, you are acknowledging that you are estimating behavior, which inherently will lead to error. However, if you are measuring behaviors that would likely be recorded inaccurately with frequency or duration because of the characteristics described before, interval recording may be a good option.

5.3 Experimental designs

Single-case experimental design is a hallmark feature of FA. Arranging environmental conditions that allow a clinician to isolate the variables responsible for changes in behavior provides stronger evidence for the function(s) of a behavior. When preparing test and control conditions, only one variable should be different so that you can isolate sources of control between and among conditions. This chapter focuses on reversal and multielement designs when conducting FA.

Reversal design

In a reversal design, you run consecutive sessions of the same condition until stable responding is achieved. You then switch to a different condition. If the behavior changes in the predicted direction during the test phase (e.g., aggression is on an increasing trend) and not the control phase (e.g., aggression remains low and stable), the challenging behavior can be attributed to that variable, because it is the only difference between the two conditions. There are many ways you can arrange conditions in a reversal design, but we are going to focus on the ABAB design.

The first thing you do in an ABAB design is try to obtain stable responding during either the control or test condition; whichever you pick would be your "A." If you were to decide to start with a control condition then you would want to see the challenging behavior occurring at low to zero rates or minimally be on a decreasing trend. Once you achieve a predictable and stable pattern then you would introduce a test condition.

You may also choose to incorporate additional test conditions within the reversal design. If you do, simply add a letter, such as "ABAC," "A" could be for control, "B" could be a test condition for attention, and "C" could be a test condition for escape.

The strengths of the reversal design are that it is the most convincing demonstration of experimental control. It may accelerate learning through repeated contact with the contingencies. In addition the probability of treatment interference is reduced by maintaining the same contingency across consecutive sessions. A limitation of the reversal design is spending more time in assessment because sessions are conducted consecutively until stable responding is evident. This concern is heightened when assessing dangerous and harmful behaviors.

Multielement design
A multielement design rapidly alternates test and control conditions. The strengths of this design are not having to wait for stability of data before changing conditions and demonstration of experimental control more quickly. This design also allows you to efficiently evaluate multiple functions if you include more than one test condition in the FA. A design limitation is potential for treatment interference because you are rapidly alternating between conditions that involve different contingencies.

5.4 Methodology
Standard functional analysis
The standard FA (e.g., Iwata et al., 1982/1994) is an improvement from indirect assessments and descriptive analysis, because it is experimental in nature. It is a good starting place if you are unsure of what function or functions are maintaining challenging behavior because it tests for social and nonsocial (automatic) functions. The methodology also can identify a function (e.g., escape) that did not appear to be relevant based upon your interviews and observations. However, the standard FA may take more time to complete.

Another limitation of the standard FA is that it does not allow for a true contingency reversal, because you are changing multiple variables within a single control condition relative to the multiple test conditions. As a result, this method has less internal validity. Another potential limitation is that the standard FA may not detect idiosyncratic variables influencing behavior such as specific establishing operations (EOs) or consequences that are influencing the person's behavior.

Children and adults may also struggle to learn the contingencies in the standard FA because of how many different contingencies are in effect across conditions. In addition, they may have a difficult time discriminating between conditions that rapidly alternate or share similar stimulus features. For example the ignore and attention conditions both involve the therapist standing farther away from the child or adult while remaining quiet.

Single-function functional analysis

The single-function test–control method is often applied within a multielement design. This approach still involves rapid alternation between conditions but only focuses on alternating between one test condition and one control condition at a time, which limits the potential for treatment interference. The design is applicable if you have strong evidence for a particular function. If you have done a few interviews and observations and cannot identify a single function for the behavior, then a standard FA might be more useful because that methodology tests for multiple functions.

A strength of the single-function test–control comparison is that it allows for a quick assessment of a potentially relevant function. Any change in the dependent variable can therefore be attributed to the one function being assessed and can be established in a short amount of time particularly when using a multielement design. In addition, testing only one function typically increases the chances that the child or adult will learn the contingency more rapidly.

Due to simplicity of the single-function FA, there are some potential limitations. Since you are comparing a single test and single control, you might overlook a function. Of course, you can always conduct subsequent phases with additional functions to examine this possibility further. If an additional function is found to be influential then we would conclude that the behavior has multiple functions.

If you are carrying out a single-function test–control FA within the context of a multielement design, the same previous limitations apply—challenges with discrimination learning and potential treatment interference. If either of these challenges becomes notable, you can change to a reversal design to address these potential confounds.

Latency functional analysis

Latency as a measurement system can be used in various FA methodologies or as a stand-alone strategy. At the start of a session the clinician starts a timer as soon as the S^D is presented, and the timer is stopped when the onset of the first instance of the target behavior occurs. Sessions end at different times depending upon the condition. During test condition sessions the session is terminated after the consequences are applied for the first occurrence of the target behavior, for example, after the therapist delivers attention for 3–5 seconds, or after demands have been removed for 20 seconds. If the target behavior does not occur, the session ends whenever the time limit for the session expires (e.g., 5 minutes). When conducting alone or control sessions within a latency FA, the clinician should wait for a predetermined amount of time after the first instance of the target behavior occurs prior to ending the session. Thomason-Sassi et al. (2011) waited 1 minute after the first instance of the target behavior to end the session, whereas our group has chosen to end sessions 20 seconds after the first instance of the target behavior occurs. As in test condition sessions, if the target behavior never occurs, the session ends when the predetermined time limit expires (e.g., 5 minutes).

One of the strengths of the latency FA is its efficiency. Since each session is terminated after the first occurrence of the target behavior, sessions can be conducted in a short amount of time, particularly when the target behavior occurs early in a session. This also is a reasonable methodology to use when evaluating individuals with high-risk behaviors. During other types of FAs, the session would not end after the first occurrence of the target behavior, which places the child or adult at greater risk of injury if the target behavior is dangerous.

Latency FAs can be particularly useful for behaviors that may only occur once such as elopement or public urination. There are also behaviors that are disruptive and require restoration of the environment (e.g., ripping materials), which are well-suited for a latency FA since the therapist can end the session and prepare the environment for the next session.

Another strength of the latency FA can be seen by comparing it to a trial-based FA. During a latency FA session, if the behavior does not occur right away, the EO can build, whereas during a trial-based FA, sessions are traditionally shorter in length (2 minutes). With a latency FA, if you conduct 10-minute sessions, you provide the opportunity for a potential EO to increase as time elapses, while also capitalizing on the ability to quickly move on to the next session if the target behavior does occur.

One of the limitations of the latency FA is that children or adults may have difficulty learning contingencies because sessions end after the first occurrence of the target behavior. There is less opportunity for variability within a session, so it may be difficult to achieve differentiation between conditions or learn more about the behavior in general. For example, you may learn more about how satiation plays a role in a behavior, such as stereotypy, by continuing to observe the child or adult repeatedly perform the behavior over a longer period of time. There is also less research about latency FAs, whereas the standard FA has been rigorously examined for decades.

Precursor functional analysis

During a precursor FA the precursor behavior to the severe challenging behavior is identified based on the interviews, direct observation, or conditional probability analysis. The precursor behavior then serves as the primary target behavior for the assessment. Researchers have used conditional probability analysis to make sure that when the precursor happens, it is generally followed by the more severe behavior.

Simply put, if there are true precursors then it would be safer to conduct an FA on those precursors than the target behavior. Presumably, the child or adult would not be engaging in the more serious behavior if the precursor behavior is quickly reinforced. It is also likely that the therapist could evoke the precursors more easily; if this is true then the FA process will be much more efficient.

The objective of a precursor FA is to prevent more intense behavior by reinforcing the less severe alternative behavior. If you have to do conditional probability analysis, you may be spending a lot of time watching someone perform the alternative behavior and the severe behavior. In essence, you may be spending more time allowing a behavior to occur, in order to create an efficient FA, which makes the overall process inefficient.

A precursor FA has the potential to be a safer alternative when analyzing dangerous challenging behavior. However, if the precursor behavior does not have the same function as the severe behavior of primary interest then you may end up conducting an inefficient FA. In such cases, you will likely end up conducting an FA with the severe behavior as the target anyway.

Trial-based functional analysis

In the context of everyday activities the trial-based FA is a good option because you can train care providers to conduct assessment in the natural environment. Data can be recorded throughout the day within the context of the individual's typical routines and without additional support.

During a trial-based FA, each trial is divided into two 2-minute segments with a control trial followed by a test trial. You should keep this order of conditions (control condition first) since research has demonstrated that conducting control sessions after a test session can result in occurrence of challenging behavior as a result of carryover effects (Bloom, Iwata, Fritz, Roscoe, & Carreau, 2011).

During control segments the EO is absent, so the reinforcer is freely available (or not present in the escape control). For example, in the attention control condition the care provider would provide noncontingent attention. The therapist would sit next to the child or adult and deliver attention. In an escape trial the EO would be absent: the aversive stimulus, of say work materials, would be absent. You would not present the work but would be sitting next to the child or adult for 2 minutes. During the second segment, you introduce the test condition. For the attention condition, you would turn yourself away from the child or adult and remove attention, and during an escape condition, you would say "Now it's time to do work" and begin presenting demands. The EO is present during the test segment. If the individual emits the behavior within those 2 minutes, you would provide the consequence. Control and test trials end upon the first occurrence of the target behavior, or after 2 minutes. The only exception is during the ignore condition when trials continue until 2 minutes expire, regardless of whether or not the target behavior is demonstrated.

During each segment, the clinician simply codes a " + " if the target behavior occurred, and a " − " if the target behavior did not occur. The percentage of trials in which the target behavior occurred for control trials and test trials is calculated and presented within a bar graph format comparing the two trials for each condition.

The trial-based FA offers several methodological advantages. Fewer resources may be needed if the care providers who typically interact with a child or adult can conduct trials. As mentioned, assessment can take place in the natural setting during everyday routines. Taking notes during the assessment can help clinicians capture potential EOs that can be incorporated into a treatment plan or built into a more specific FA at a later time.

The trial-based FA is useful if you are busy in session rooms or if you do not want to remove the child or adult from her/his typical setting. This provides an element of efficiency that is minimally disruptive to the client's and clinical team's routine particularly if a clear function is identified. The design also allows more team members to become skilled in conducting certain elements of FA and could make further training in FA more efficient at a later time if you wanted to train particular team members in additional aspects of FA training. If no clear function emerges, you may still have useful information about EOs and reinforcers that helps you build a more refined FA.

There are several disadvantages when deciding whether or not to conduct a trial-based FA. Uncontrolled variables may interfere with experimental control should a peer give attention by looking at the child or adult or someone commenting about challenging behavior (e.g., "Tell him to be quiet"). You also have limited exposure to the EOs given the short segment of time. Aggregated data might mask temporal patterns of responding, because you are combining everything across assessment sessions into a single bar for that particular condition trial. Perhaps the biggest limitation of this approach is that in its traditional form the trial-based FA is nonexperimental. However, this limitation can be addressed by graphing each trial as a data point in a multielement design rather than aggregating the data into a bar graph. Lastly, analysis may be limited because data are coded as either occurrence or nonoccurrence per segment. The analysis of trends and variability in your data are not available with this type of data collection.

Extended alone/ignore condition

The extended alone/ignore condition involves conducting one long session or multiple alone sessions that are shorter in duration back to back. This format allows for the observation of extinction of the challenging behavior if it is maintained by social consequences or continued high rates of behavior if it is maintained by automatic reinforcement. The design is a good first option if you suspect automatic reinforcement as the function of behavior and can also help one to clarify undifferentiated data obtained from a standard FA.

When determining the length of extended alone/ignore session, you may choose to incorporate a longer session (e.g., 30 minutes) if the rate of behavior is high and therapist presence might signal available reinforcement for other behavior. For example a child or adult may start making requests when the therapist enters the room. If the therapist then leaves, denied access to tangibles may trigger challenging behavior if there is a tangible function. In contrast, if you are running 30-minute sessions, you may find that challenging behavior decreases due to satiation or fatigue. If this were to be the case, you may wish to break the sessions up by taking a short break in between, such as going for a walk.

The chief limitation of an extended alone/ignore session is lack of experimental control. In addition, this methodology does not allow you to test for specific social and nonsocial functions. As a result, you may find a clear automatic function and design a treatment, only to later find out that there are relevant social functions that also need to be addressed.

If you do find that the behavior is maintained by automatic reinforcement, it may be necessary to examine what aspect of the consequence is maintaining the behavior. Is it visual? Tactile? Auditory? Your analysis may allow you to determine whether automatic reinforcement is maintaining the behavior, but more information will typically need to be ascertained for an effective treatment to be designed. Consider a child or adult whose fire alarm−pulling behavior is maintained by automatic reinforcement. It could be the relevant stimulus characteristics that are motivating this behavior are the flashing lights or the noise produced when the alarm is triggered, or perhaps it is the tactile consequences associated with pulling the lever. If the consequences maintaining behavior were solely tactile in nature, the child or adult might be able to request time to pull the lever of a deactivated fire alarm pull station that can be carried across settings. However, if the noise made by the alarm was the motivating consequence, this type of intervention would likely have no impact on behavior.

Interview-informed synthesized contingency analysis

The interview-informed synthesized contingency analysis (IISCA) (Hanley et al., 2014; Jessel, Hanley, & Ghaemmaghami, 2016) is a type of FA in which the most likely reinforcers maintaining behavior are determined during interviews and observations. These potential reinforcers are then presented together following the target behavior in the test condition. In the control condition the reinforcers are freely available, or if there are negative reinforcers that are believed to be relevant, they are absent.

The IISCA may aid the clinician in determining a function more quickly. This approach may also better approximate the conditions in the natural environment that evoke the target behavior. There has been increasing empirical support that this type of FA can accurately identify functions and lead to the development of effective treatments in a more efficient manner than traditional FAs.

There are, however, several potential disadvantages associated with IISCA, namely, that this method is less experimentally sound since variables are not isolated when examining change in the dependent variable. It is possible that additional variables may be deemed as relevant when they are not (e.g., a teacher provides attention and toys, but only attention is truly maintaining the behavior). Misinterpretation of IISCA-produced data could result in treatment plans that require more effort and resources than necessary. Another challenge is that it can be difficult to establish a reliable interview method such that different clinicians may generate contradictory hypotheses when evaluating the same child or adult.

5.5 Reproducible figures and forms

Name: _____   Date: _____

1) Which of the FA methodologies would be best to use when a child or adult may need multiple learning trials to discriminate the contingencies of your FA or when the function of the behavior is unclear based on your interview and observations (1pt)?
    a. Latency based FA
    b. Standard FA
    c. Trial-based FA
    d. Single Function FA

2) Describe the difference between a reversal and multielement experimental design (1pt):

3) Discuss two limitations of a standard FA (2pts):

4) In a latency based FA, what should the therapist do after the target behavior occurs in a play or control condition (1pt)?

5) Which of the following is not a strength of a trial-based FA (1pt)?
    a. Fewer resources are required to conduct it
    b. This methodology may allow you to capture idiosyncratic EOs
    c. Allows you to conduct sessions in a discontinuous manner
    d. Session by session trends enhance interpretation of the data

Figure 5.1 Measurement, experimental design, methodology quiz.

6) Joe engages in stereotypy in the form of hand flapping. You hypothesize the behavior is maintained by automatic reinforcement. Which FA methodology would allow you to test this hypothesis most efficiently (1pt)?

7) Sally engages in severe SIB in the form of biting of her wrists. Her clinician approaches you to discuss carrying out a functional analysis. The clinician is thinking of using a traditional functional analysis methodology with 5 min sessions, but would like to know if you agree that this would be the best method. If not, the clinician would like to know what FA methodology would you suggest and why? What would your feedback be (3 pts)?

FA Method: Traditional   or   Other: _____

Rationale:

Feedback to Clinician:

8) Which experimental design would be best to use if your biggest concern is treatment interference (1pt)?
    a. Reversal
    b. Multielement
    c. Changing Criterion

Figure 5.1 Continued

70   Functional Analysis

   d. Trial-based

9) What are two limitations of the precursor FA method (2pts)?

10) You have chosen a latency methodology and measurement system for your FA. The therapist who will be measuring latency knows when to start and stop the timer as it relates to measuring the target behavior. However, they are confused as to when to start and stop the session timer (i.e., when should the sessions be terminated). Your colleague asks you when to start their session timer and when to stop it for both social test conditions, alone/ignore conditions, and control conditions. What would your response be (4pts)?

Start for Test and Control Conditions (1 pt):

Stop for Social Test Conditions (1 pt):

Stop for Control and Alone/Ignore Conditions (2 pts):

11) Larry engages in mouthing of objects. Sometimes he mouths objects for long periods of time (e.g., 2 min), other times he repeatedly mouths different objects for short durations and brief interresponse times (e.g., picks one up, mouths it, puts it down, picks up a different item, mouths it). The clinician is using a standard FA to evaluate Larry's mouthing of objects. What measurement system would be best for analyzing this behavior (1pt)?

12) The following graph depicts data for which type of FA (1pt)?

Figure 5.1 Continued

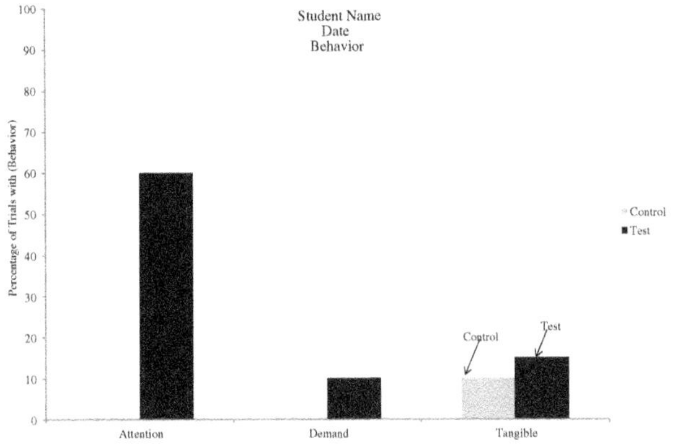
Student Name
Date
Behavior
Percentage of Trials with (Behavior)
100
90
80
70
60
50
40
30
20
10
0
Control
Test
Attention
Demand
Tangible
Control
Test

13) Your colleague, Samantha, is working with a client who displays severe aggression, property destruction, and SIB. She believes they are all maintained by the same function, although property destruction tends to occur first. She is considering conducting a functional analysis in which all three of these behaviors are considered target behaviors. Should she measure all three behaviors, and if so, how might you suggest she do this? Alternatively, should she only measure one or two of the behaviors, and if so, which one(s) (2 pts)?

Figure 5.1 Continued

14) In the spaces provided, write the measurement system you think is best and explain why (3pts):

   a. Dangerous self-injury, with a clear onset and offset:

   b. Self-restraint (tucking hands underneath clothes, other body parts) that tends to occur for long durations:

   c. Throwing objects:

Total Score (out of 24 pts): _____

Figure 5.1 Continued

Measurement, experimental design, methodology   73

1) Which of the FA methodologies would be best to use when a client may need multiple learning trials to discriminate the contingencies of your FA or when the function of the behavior is unclear based on your interview and observations (1pt)?
    a. Latency based FA
    b. *Standard FA*
    c. Trial-based FA
    d. Single Function FA

2) Describe the difference between a reversal and multielement experimental design (1pt):

    A multielement design involves rapidly alternating between multiple test and control conditions, whereas a reversal design involves running consecutive sessions of the same test or control condition until stability (or predictability) of the data is achieved prior to changing conditions.

3) Discuss two limitations of a standard FA (2pts):

    Any of the two answers below are sufficient (1pt per response)

    1) There is the potential for treatment interference given the rapid alternation between multiple conditions
    2) The client may have challenges discriminating between conditions given the rapid alternation between conditions and multiple contingencies in the assessment
    3) There are multiple differences between the test and control conditions which prevents you from isolating an independent variable as the sole difference between the two conditions
    4) Because you have a control condition with multiple test conditions for fixed session durations, the assessment can be more time consuming than other types of functional analyses

4) In a latency based FA, what should the therapist do after the target behavior occurs in a play or control condition (1pt)?

    Wait 20-30 seconds prior to terminating the session to avoid adventitious reinforcement

Figure 5.2 Answer key for measurement, experimental design, methodology quiz.

5) Which of the following is not a strength of a trial-based FA (1pt)?
   a. Fewer resources are required to conduct it
   b. This methodology may allow you to capture idiosyncratic EOs
   c. Allows you to conduct sessions in a discontinuous manner
   d. *Session by session trends enhance interpretation of the data*

6) Joe engages in stereotypy in the form of hand flapping. You hypothesize the behavior is maintained by automatic reinforcement. Which FA methodology would allow you to test this hypothesis most efficiently (1pt)?

   Extended alone condition

7) Sally engages in severe SIB in the form of biting of her wrists. Her clinician approaches you to discuss carrying out a functional analysis. The clinician is thinking of using a traditional functional analysis methodology with 5 min sessions, but would like to know if you agree that this would be the best method. If not, the clinician would like to know what FA methodology would you suggest and why? What would your feedback be (3 pts)?

   FA Method: Traditional   or   Other:

   _____

   Scoring the Response

   Agree or Disagree (1pt)?
   Tell the clinician that you do not agree the standard FA is the best approach

   Rationale (1pt):
   A method other than a traditional functional analysis is preferable in this situation given the severity of SIB and the amount of session time that would be necessary to get interpretable results. The increased session time increases the risk of injury for an individual with this type of challenging behavior.

   An alternative method that allows for more efficient analysis, such as a single function FA, or a latency based or precursor FA would be preferable.

Figure 5.2 Continued

Given the health and safety risks associated with severe SIB, the clinician should select a methodology and design that allows for an efficient analysis of SIB, or an evaluation of an alternative, yet functionally related topography.

Feedback to Clinician (1pt):
The primary feedback given to the clinician should be that the severity and risk of the target behavior should influence his or her selection of an FA methodology.

Encourage the clinician to focus on the interview and observation process to aid in the development of a specific hypothesis that can be assessed using a test-control multielement design.

If the clinician suspects multiple functions, or is unclear about function after taking these pre-assessment measures, then a latency design would also be a good choice since it would include multiple test conditions as in a standard FA, but the session length is decreased during conditions if the target behavior occurs.

A precursor FA may also be a good option if a reliable precursor to severe SIB can be identified prior to designing the FA.

8) Which experimental design would be best to use if your biggest concern is treatment interference (1pt)?
    a. *Reversal*
    b. Multielement
    c. Changing criterion
    d. Trial-based

9) What are two limitations of the precursor FA method (2pts)?

Any of the two answers below are sufficient (1 pt per response)

  1) Identifying a reliable precursor prior to designing the FA can be time-consuming; the time spent identifying one might be better spent in FA session time
  2) The functions of the precursor behavior and problem behavior may not match
  3) The methods for identifying precursors are not well-established and validated

Figure 5.2 Continued

76 Functional Analysis

10) You have chosen a latency methodology and measurement system for your FA. The therapist who will be measuring latency knows when to start and stop the timer as it relates to measuring the target behavior. However, they are confused as to when to start and stop the session timer (i.e., when should the sessions be terminated). Your colleague asks you when to start their session timer and when to stop it for both social test conditions, alone/ignore conditions, and control conditions. What would your response be (4pts)?

Start for Test and Control Conditions (1 pt): *The therapist should start his or her timer immediately after presenting the S^d*

Stop for Social Test Conditions (1 pt): *The therapist should stop the timer as soon as the operational definition for the target behavior is met during test conditions*

Stop for Control and Alone/Ignore Conditions (2 pts): *20 s after the target behavior has occurred for the control condition and for alone/ignore conditions*

11) Larry engages in mouthing of objects. Sometimes he mouths objects for long periods of time (e.g., 2 min), other times he repeatedly mouths different objects for short durations and brief interresponse times (e.g., picks one up, mouths it, puts it down, picks up a different item, mouths it). The clinician is using a standard FA to evaluate Larry's mouthing of objects. What measurement system would be best for analyzing this behavior (1pt)?

Duration would not be a good choice because it would be difficult to keep track of given the frequency of the behavior and short interresponse times. The clinician could use frequency as a measurement system but should acknowledge this might be difficult given the rapid nature of the behavior. An interval sampling method may be the best option as long as the clinician uses a short interval (e.g., 5 seconds).

12) The following graph depicts data for which type of FA (1pt)?

Figure 5.2 Continued

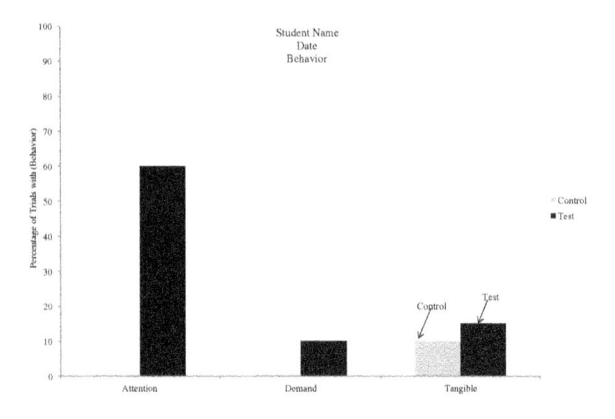

Trial-based FA

13) Your colleague, Samantha, is working with a client who displays severe aggression, property destruction, and SIB. She believes they are all maintained by the same function, although property destruction tends to occur first. She is considering conducting a functional analysis in which all three of these behaviors are considered target behaviors. Should she measure all three behaviors, and if so, how might you suggest she do this? Alternatively, should she only measure one or two of the behaviors, and if so, which one(s) (2 pts)?

1 point for suggesting to select 1 target behavior

1 point for identifying property destruction or first behavior to occur as the target behavior

You should recommend to Samantha that she should select one behavior as the target behavior since measurement of multiple target behaviors has been demonstrated in the literature to lead to a greater likelihood of undifferentiated results.

Samantha could select property destruction as the target behavior since it tends to occur first. Alternatively, she could make the first of these behaviors that occurs in session as the target behavior.

Figure 5.2 Continued

14) In the spaces provided, write the measurement system you think is best and explain why (3pts):

   a. Dangerous self-injury, with a clear onset and offset: *Frequency (it is easily countable); Latency (may be a good representation of response strength) – the trainee may also indicate that in addition to using latency as a measurement system, a latency FA methodology would be a good choice as well.*

   b. Self-restraint (tucking hands underneath clothes, other body parts) that tends to occur for long durations:
   Frequency may not provide the variability necessary to differentiate data across conditions and may not provide an accurate measure of the behavior.

   Duration would be a good choice to capture this behavior since duration is a very relevant dimension as the behavior occurs for long stretches of time. Interval recording is also a good option, although continuous measures are preferred.

   c. Throwing objects:
   Throwing objects is likely a very countable behavior so frequency would be a good choice

   Latency may also be a good measurement system if once the client starts to engage in property destruction, he or she continues for long durations

Total Score (out of 24 pts): _____

Figure 5.2 Continued

CHAPTER 6

Graphing, graph interpretation, managing undifferentiated data

6.1 Overview of training procedures

The fifth level of the curriculum marks the start of postanalysis, or said another way, the skills clinicians need to have after the assessment (or at least after part of the assessment) has been conducted. Following a functional analysis (FA), clinicians need to be able to graph the data, interpret data to determine one or more functions, and make decisions about next steps in the assessment process if the data are undifferentiated.

The first component of the curriculum begins by distributing the handout, *task analysis for creating graphs with Microsoft Excel 2016* (Fig. 6.1), which provides task analyses for creating reversal, multielement, and trial-based graphs. Trainees are asked to use the guide to create the graphs demonstrated within the task analysis, and the trainers answer any questions they might have along the way. This part of training is self-directed, and we have found it to be very effective, even when trainees have little to no experience graphing. Following the tutorial, trainees are given the *graphing quiz* that includes data sets for each type of FA graph (see Fig. 6.2). Trainees complete their graphs during a training session and, when they are done, email their graphs to the trainer for scoring. Graphs produced by trainees can be compared to the *answer key for graphing quiz* (Fig. 6.3), and graphing accuracy is measured using the *scoring rubrics for FA graphs* that are displayed in Fig. 6.4.

Once trainees demonstrate competence graphing data, instruction is provided in graph interpretation. We originally used methods of interpretation described by Hagopian et al. (1997) that we have revised for various types of data sets when training employees (Chok, Shlesinger, Studer, & Bird, 2012). However, over the time we favored the

Reversal Graphs

Entering Data

1. Enter labels for Sessions (in cell A1)
2. Enter labels for each of your conditions in the first cell of adjacent columns
   a. E.g., Column B1 = Attention
   b. E.g., Column C1 = Escape
   c. E.g., Column D1 = Play
3. Enter the label "Condition Lines" in the next column (e.g., E1)

After you enter these labels, your database should look like the picture below:

A	B	C	D	E
Session #	Attention	Escape	Play	Condition Lines

4. Enter in numbers for each of the sessions in the A column cells below (e.g., 1, 2, 3, 4…)
5. Enter in the corresponding data in the Attention, Escape, and Play cells – leave cells in which there is no data blank (do not enter zeros)
   a. Attention Values to Enter: 0, 0, 0, 0
   b. Escape Values to Enter: 8, 9, 10, 12
   c. Play Values to Enter: 0, 0, 0, 0
   d. Escape Values to Enter: 10, 12, 10, 11
   e. Play Values to Enter: 0, 0, 0, 0
6. Insert two Condition Line values in the Session # column at 0.5 values between changes in conditions
   a. E.g., Our Attention sessions stopped on Session 4, and Play sessions began on Session 5, so you would add in 4.5 and 4.5 under the Sessions column between the 4 and 5 values
   b. In the Condition Lines column, enter the values of 0 for the first 4.5 session, and then round up from the highest data value to determine what number you will list for the second 4.5 session (in this case the highest data value is 12, so we can round up to 15)

Figure 6.1 Task analysis for creating graphs in Microsoft Excel 2016.

traditional use of visual analysis which was being used to interpret other graphs agency-wide. Therefore this component of training incorporates principles of visual analysis described in textbooks such as Cooper et al. (2007) and Gast and Leford (2014). Instruction is provided using a slideshow presentation and then performance is measured using a quiz, which can be found in Fig. 6.5 (*graph interpretation quiz*). Trainee responses are scored using the *answer key for graph interpretation quiz* (Fig. 6.6).

Clinicians conducting FAs also are likely to encounter data sets in which a clear function cannot be determined because the data are undifferentiated. Therefore we also include instruction

After you enter the data, your spreadsheet should look like the one below:

	A	B	C	D	E
1	Session #	Attention	Escape	Play	Condition Lines
2	1	0			
3	2	0			
4	3	0			
5	4	0			
6	4.5				0
7	4.5				15
8	5		8		
9	6		9		
10	7		10		
11	8		12		
12	8.5				0
13	8.5				15
14	9			0	
15	10			0	
16	11			0	
17	12			0	
18	12.5				0
19	12.5				15
20	13		10		
21	14		12		
22	15		10		
23	16		11		
24	16.5				0
25	16.5				15
26	17			0	
27	18			0	
28	19			0	
29	20			0	

Creating the Graph

1. Highlight all of your data, including column labels, click on the Insert tab, and select the "Scatter" option in the Charts area, then select "Scatter with Straight Lines and Markers" option.

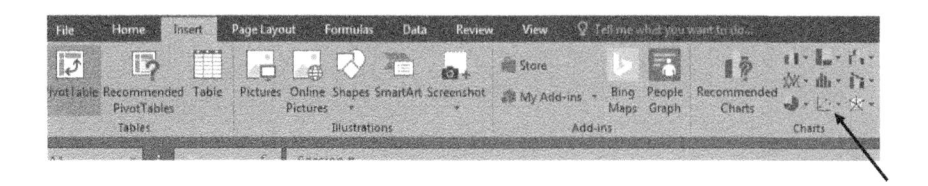

Figure 6.1 Continued.

regarding additional steps that can be taken when data are high and undifferentiated (Vollmer, Marcus, Ringdahl, & Roane, 1995) and when data are low and undifferentiated (Chok et al., 2012; Hanley, 2012; Hanley et al., 2003). Instruction about how to proceed when data are undifferentiated is provided using a slideshow presentation, and then performance is measured using a quiz that can be found in Fig. 6.7 (*managing undifferentiated data quiz*).

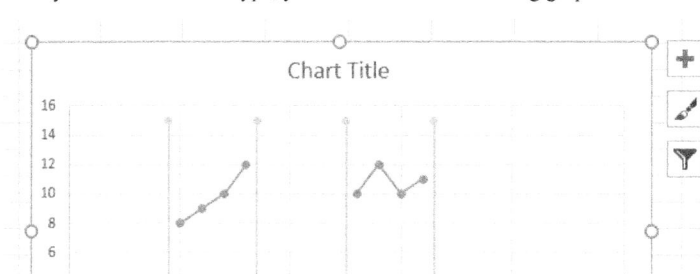

Once you select this chart type, you should see the following graph:

2. Click on the graph and select "Move Chart," then select "New sheet," type in "FA Reversal Graph" and click the OK button. This will move your chart to a separate sheet and make it easier to work with.

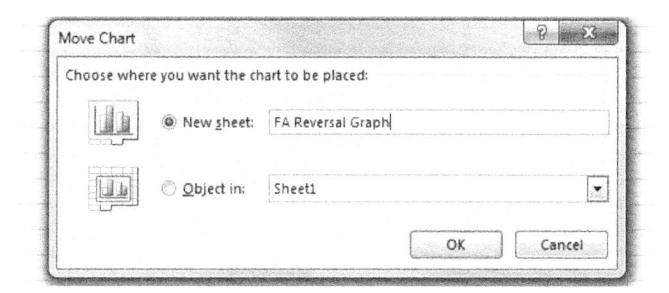

Figure 6.1 Continued.

Trainee responses for the quiz are scored using the *answer key for managing undifferentiated data quiz* (Fig. 6.8).

Training steps for Level 6
Graphing
1. Trainer conducts slideshow presentation and trainees are given the handout, *task analysis for creating graphs with Microsoft Excel 2016* (Fig. 6.1), that provides step-by-step instructions about how to construct graphs.
2. Trainee takes the *graphing quiz* (Fig. 6.2), and graphs are compared to the *answer key for graphing quiz* (Fig. 6.3).

Editing the Graph

There are a few edits to the graph which are good to make so that it looks more like the graphs conventionally seen in the field of behavior analysis.

HINT: While you are carrying out the steps below, there are a few useful commands Windows will perform when the keyboard buttons are pressed sequentially (e.g., pressing and holding the CTRL key, then pressing a letter button):

CTRL + Z = undoes any action; good to use if you make a mistake

CRTL + Y = Repeats an action you just made; good to use if you performed a menu command and would like to do the same action for another part of your graph

CRTL + C = Copies the information selected

CTRL + V = Pastes the information that was selected

CTRL + A = Highlights all information on the working area of the screen; good for when you want to highlight individual parts of your graph and group them as a whole so you can then move one integrated object around on the screen or paste it to another working area.

1. Click on the vertical gray gridlines (blue circles should appear on the top and bottom of these lines if you selected them) and hit the "Delete" button on your keyboard

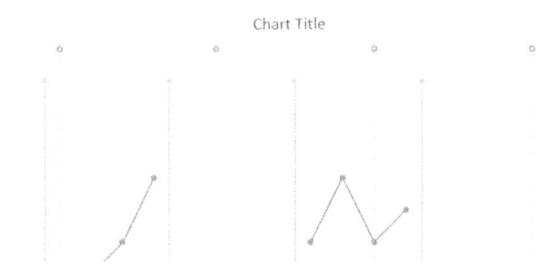

Figure 6.1 Continued.

3. Performance is measured using the *scoring rubric for creating graphs* data sheets as displayed in Fig. 6.4.

Graph interpretation
1. Trainer conducts slideshow presentation on graph interpretation.
2. Trainee takes the *graph interpretation quiz*—Fig. 6.5.
3. Quizzes are scored using the *answer key for graph interpretation quiz* (Fig. 6.6).

Undifferentiated data
1. Trainer conducts slideshow presentation on managing undifferentiated data.

2. Do the same for the horizontal gray gridlines

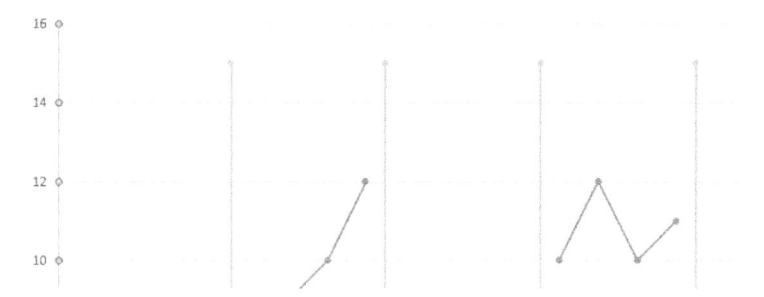

3. Your graph should now look like the picture below

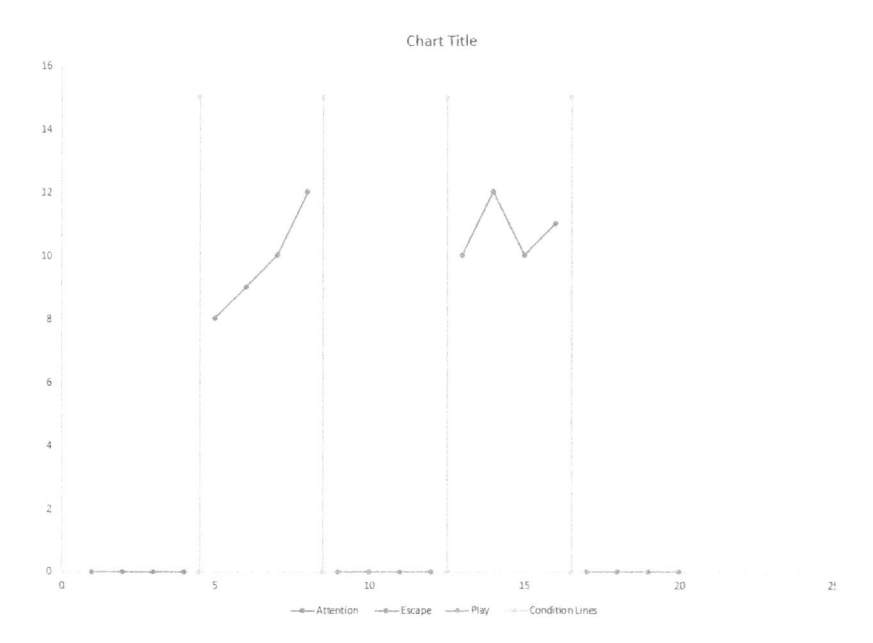

Figure 6.1 Continued.

2. Trainee takes the *managing undifferentiated data quiz*—Fig. 6.7.
3. Quizzes are scored using the *answer key for managing undifferentiated data quiz* (Fig. 6.8).

Criteria to pass Level 5
- Score of 90% or higher on graphing quiz
- Score of 90% or higher on graph interpretation quiz
- Score of 90% or higher on managing undifferentiated data quiz

4. You will notice your y-axis value is higher than the highest condition line value. Go back to your data sheet in Excel and change the upper value of your condition lines to 16, so they are even with your upper y-axis value. This step has been included so you know how to make the adjustment if need be – on future graphs, rounding up to an even number may eliminate the need to perform this step.

```
Condition Lines

    0
    16


    0
    16


    0
    16


    0
    16
```

Figure 6.1 Continued.

6.2 Graphing

Once data have been collected, the next step is to create graphs that depict the FA results. Although there are many ways to graph FA data, we have included some recommended standard features to help make the interpretation process more efficient. All graphs depicting FA results should include the following:

- A title
- Different symbols for each of your conditions
  - Open symbols (white fill) for control conditions
  - Closed symbols (filled in) for test conditions
- Labeled *y*-axis
- Labeled *x*-axis

Sessions go on the *x*-axis (unless it is a trial-based graph), whereas the targeted problem behavior and measurement system goes on the *y*-axis (e.g., latency to aggression). When presenting a graph, it is important to not only draw attention to the essential elements of the graph (e.g., type of FA, *y*-axis label, *x*-axis label, trend of the data

5. Click on the x-axis on the graph tab and select "Format Axis"
    a. Change the Maximum Value to 20, so it matches the number of sessions you conducted
    b. When you are done, your graph should look like the picture below

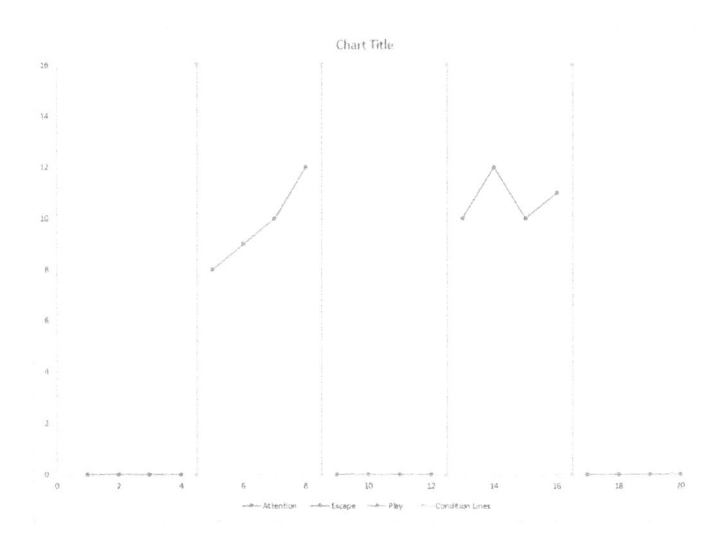

6. Removing references to "Condition Lines" as a data path. The condition lines are not an actual data series so delete them from the legend on the bottom of the screen and remove the data symbols attached to the condition lines
    a. Deleting from Legend
        i. Click on the Legend at the bottom of the screen – you will notice the whole Legend is selected
        ii. Click on the "Conditions Line" label in the Legend so that only that portion is selected
        iii. Hit the delete key on your keyboard

Figure 6.1 Continued.

path), but also the rationale behind your work. Make sure to give your audience a context for your findings, or else it will be difficult for them to understand the relevance of your work. For example, provide information to the audience about the person you assessed, why his or her behavior is socially significant, and why you chose the key elements of your FA (e.g., type of FA, measurement system, experimental design).

Graphing, graph interpretation, managing undifferentiated data   87

b. Removing symbols for condition lines
    i. Left click on one of the yellow circle symbols attached to a condition line
    ii. You will notice a few of the yellow circles will be selected because of the blue circles that appear on them (if this does not work, click outside of the graph area and try again)

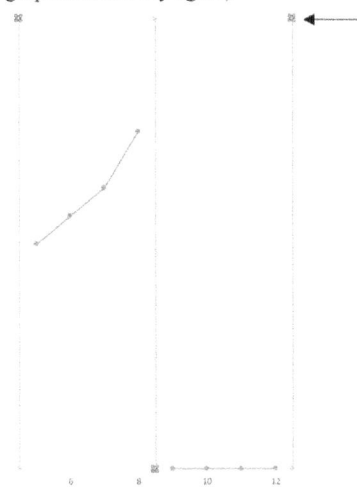

    iii. Right click on one of the yellow circles with a blue outline and select "Format Data Series"
        1. Left click on the "Fill and Line" symbol
        2. Left click on "Marker"

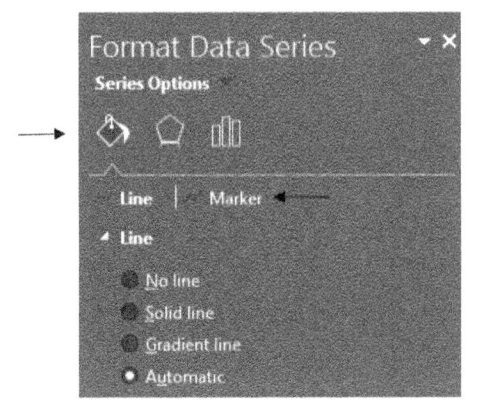

Figure 6.1 Continued.

6.3 Reproducible figures for graphing

The figures for this section are the quiz used to measure graphing skills, along with the answer key. These figures can be photocopied for use during training sessions.

88 Functional Analysis

   3. Select "Marker Options" then select "None"
 iv. Your graph should now look like the picture below

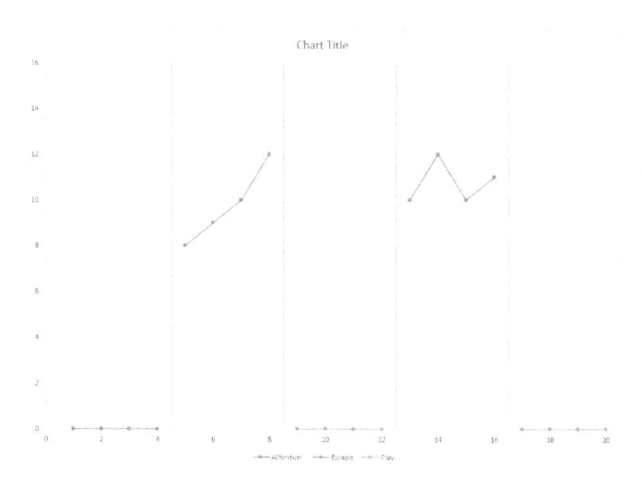

[Chart showing Attention, Escape, Play data paths]

7. We are now going to make two changes that will make the graph look more conventional when displaying FA data in a reversal design: 1) Selecting a unique symbol for each FA condition; 2) Removing color so your graph is black and white
   a. Symbols
      i. We suggest using open (filled with the color white) symbols for control/play conditions and solid (filled with the color black) symbols for test conditions. If you consistently graph in this manner, it may help your audience more readily discriminate test conditions from control conditions
      ii. Left click on the Attention data path and select "Format Series"
         1. Left click on "Fill & Line"
            a. Select "Solid line" then select the color black from the "Color" option below
            b. You can now click on the Escape data path and hit the "CTRL" and "Y" buttons simultaneously. This is the "Redo" function and will make the Escape data path black.
            c. Left click on the Play data path and hit "CTRL" + "Y"
            d. All data paths should now be black
            e. Also select the area just above a condition line and hit "CTRL" + "Y" to make those lines black as well
            f. Your graph should now look like the picture below

Figure 6.1 Continued.

6.4 Graph interpretation

After graphing FA data the clinician will need to interpret those data. The key variables to consider when interpreting a graph are how many data points are depicted, the variability of the data, and the trend and

Graphing, graph interpretation, managing undifferentiated data 89

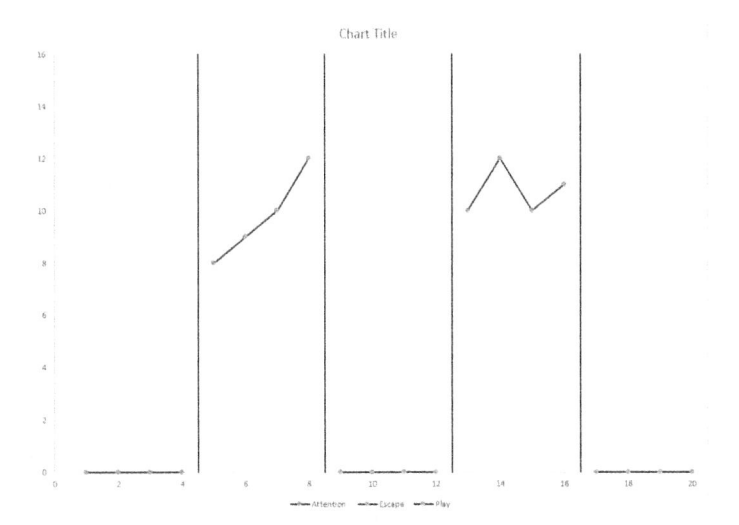

[Chart: Chart Title with Attention, Escape, Play data series]

b. Changing Data Symbols
   i. Select the Attention condition data series by left clicking on one of the data points and selecting "Format Data Series"
   ii. Click on "Fill & Line" and "Marker," then "Marker Options"
   iii. Select a unique symbol (e.g., a square), then change the "Size" to a 6 or 7
   iv. Under "Fill" select "Solid Fill," then select black as the color
   v. Under the "Border" section, select "No line"
   vi. Repeat these steps for the Escape condition symbols (you can leave them as circles) and the Play condition symbols (just remember to select "Solid Fill" then the color white for these). For the Play condition symbols you also need to select "Border – Solid Line" and change the color to black
c. Clarifying Legend data symbols
   i. It may be difficult to see the symbols in your legend
   ii. One way to make the symbols easier to see is to decrease the thickness of the line going through them
      1. Click on the Legend, then click on one of the Legend entries (e.g., Play condition) so that only that entry is highlighted

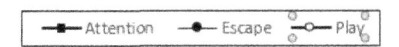

[Legend: Attention — Escape — Play]

Figure 6.1 Continued.

the level of the data set. When interpreting FA data, comparisons are made between the control condition and the various test conditions. Test conditions are not compared against each other because many things differ between these test conditions.

2. In the "Border" section, decrease the "Width" value to 0.5

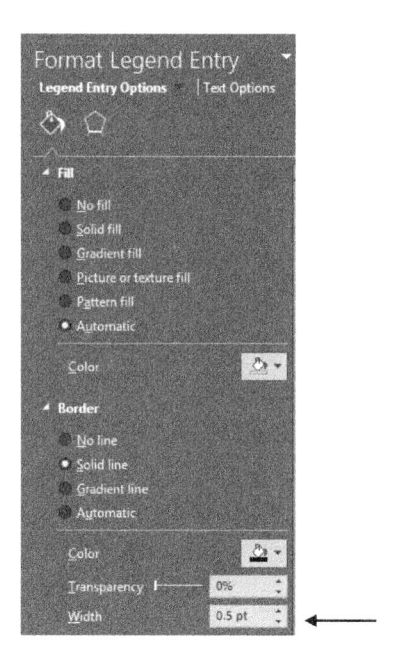

3. This will decrease the thickness of the line crossing through the symbol, so the symbol becomes more visible

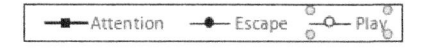

4. You can also make the symbols for the condition stand out more by increasing the font size
    a. Select a condition in the Legend, and then right click, and select "Font" and change the font to 14

Figure 6.1 Continued.

Visual analysis

When interpreting graphs, a visual analysis between the conditions is performed. With regard to the number of data points, the more data points that are represented, the more confidence you can have in your interpretation. Analysis of the stability and variability of the data, along with the level and trend of the data between adjacent phases and conditions, and across similar phases is also important. Fewer data

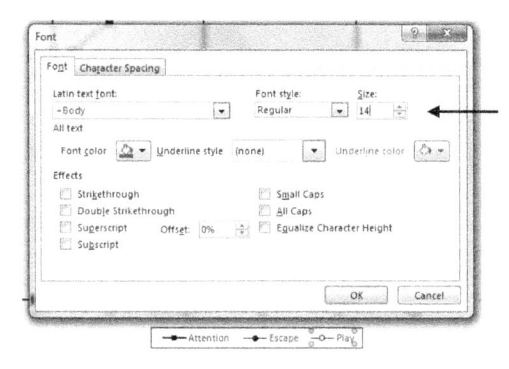

Graphing, graph interpretation, managing undifferentiated data   91

b. Click on each of the other conditions and hit "CTRL" + "Y" to redo this effect
c. Your Legend should now look like the picture below

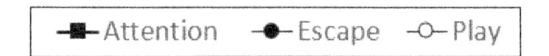

5. Move the Legend so there is room for the x-axis label
   a. Left click on the Legend
   b. Select "Format Legend"
   c. Under "Legend Options – Legend Position" select "Right" and then uncheck the box "Show the Legend without Overlapping the Box"

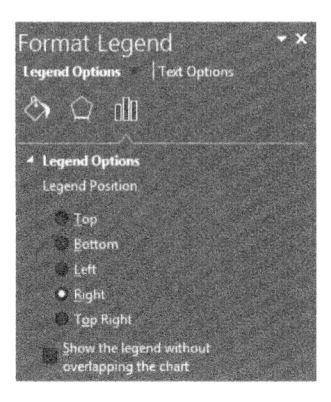

d. Change the "Chart Title" by clicking in it and typing the name of your FA (e.g., "Functional Analysis of Aggression")
e. Removing Borders

Figure 6.1 Continued.

i. Click near (but not on) some data points so you can remove the border in the plot area. Select "No Line" in the Border menu

ii. Click outside of the plot area (somewhere above the top of your condition lines) – you should see a menu labeled "Format Chart Area" appear – select "No Line" in the Border area

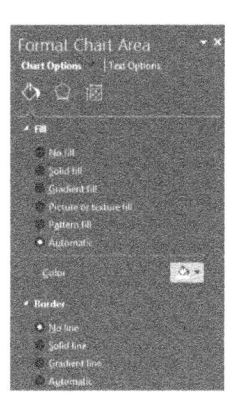

Figure 6.1 Continued.

points are needed in subsequent replications if the same level and trend are present in earlier treatment conditions.

High variability suggests that the clinician does not have very good control over the environment. In other words, there are other variables influencing behavior besides what the clinician has decided to manipulate. Just like in a laboratory, the clinician should be carefully and consistently making the same changes between conditions while holding all other variables constant.

f. Your graph should now look like the picture below

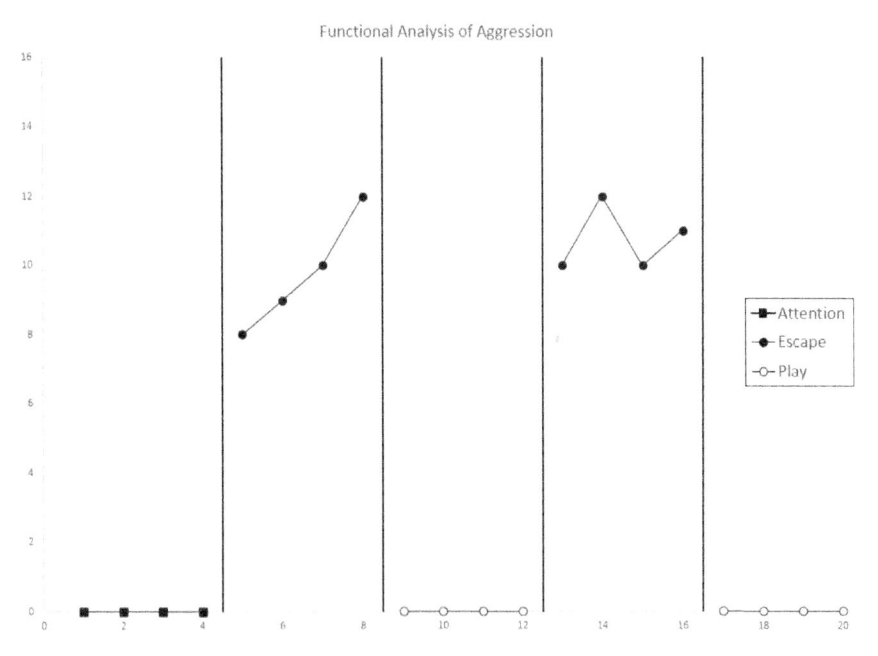

Functional Analysis of Aggression

8. Adding labels for the y- and x-axis
   a. Left click on your graph
   b. Left click on the "Design" tab in the menu
   c. Left click on the "Add Chart Element" to access the drop down menu

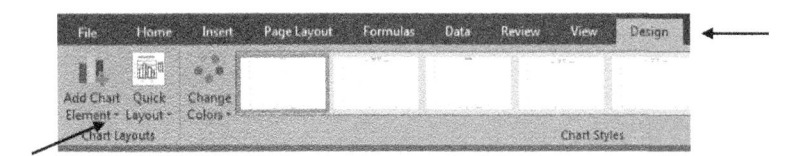

   d. Select "Axis Titles" then "Primary Horizontal"

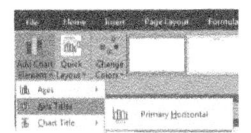

Figure 6.1 Continued.

There are likely going to be conditions that are outside of the clinician's control, such as the child or adult having a headache, jaw pain, an unsettled stomach, or being tired from a poor night's sleep. If these

94 Functional Analysis

   e. A title for the x-axis will appear, left click in the box, erase the stock title and type in "Sessions (5 min)" to indicate you are displaying consecutive sessions that were 5 min in length (which we are assuming for the purpose of this exercise)
   f. Highlight the text and increase the font size to 14
   g. Select the "Primary Vertical" from the "Axis Titles" menu and repeat these steps, using "Frequency of Aggression" as the title

Your graph is now complete and should look like the picture below:

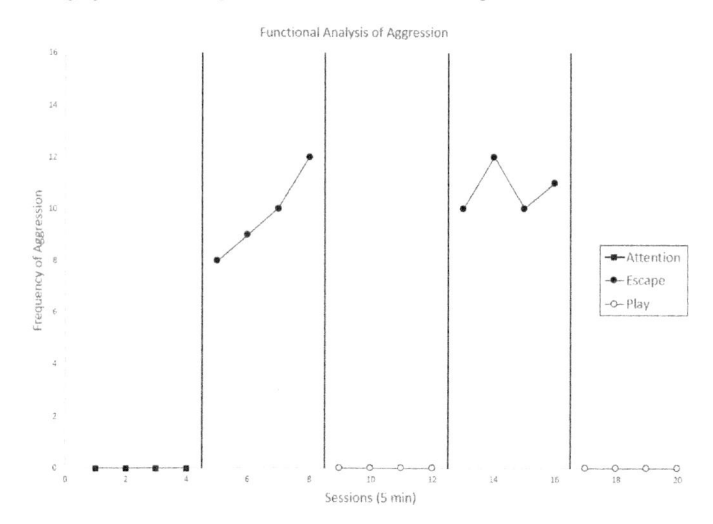

[Graph: Functional Analysis of Aggression, showing Attention, Escape, and Play conditions plotted across Sessions (5 min) on the x-axis and Frequency of Aggression on the y-axis]

Multielement Graphs

Labeling and Creating New Data Sheets

1. Right click on the tab titled, "Sheet 1" and select "Rename"
2. Type in the title, "FA Reversal Data"
3. Then left click the "+" button to create a new sheet

[Image: tabs showing "FA Reversal Graph", "Sheet1", and a "+" button]

4. Rename this new sheet "FA Multielement Data"

Figure 6.1 Continued.

are relevant variables, there will likely be increased variability in the data set. This is because variables are changing that the clinician did not anticipate changing or that the clinician did not identify as relevant. Most of the time, variability makes interpretation more difficult. Stable data are generally easier to interpret. If variability is high, the clinician may need to collect data longer to establish a predictable pattern.

Entering Data

1. Enter labels for Sessions (in cell A1)
2. Enter labels for each of your conditions in the first cell of adjacent columns
    a. E.g., Column B1 = Attention
    b. E.g., Column C1 = Escape
    c. E.g., Column D1 = Play
3. Enter in the numbers 1 through 12 to notate there were 12 sessions worth of data
4. Enter in the following data for each condition
    a. Attention
        i. Session 1 = 6
        ii. Session 4 = 10
        iii. Session 8 = 12
        iv. Session 11 = 12
    b. Escape
        i. Session 3 = 9
        ii. Session 6 = 8
        iii. Session 9 = 11
        iv. Session 12 = 13
    c. Play
        i. Session 2 = 2
        ii. Session 5 = 1
        iii. Session 7 = 0
        iv. Session 10 = 0

Creating the Graph

1. Highlight all of your data, including column labels, click on the Insert tab, and select the "Scatter" option in the Charts area, then select "Scatter with Straight Lines and Markers" option.

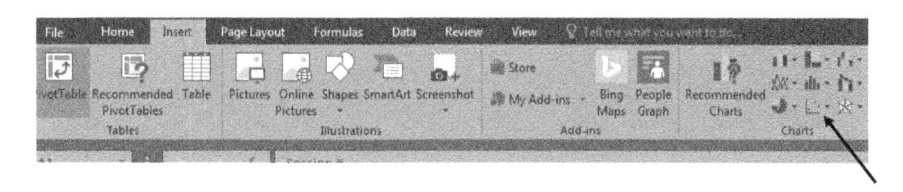

Figure 6.1 Continued.

Given that some things may change that are outside of the clinician's control, it is very important to ensure consistency in the elements of each condition that are within the clinician's control. For example, if attention is a relevant variable, the precision with which the clinician applies attention contingent upon the target response will likely influence the degree of variability. Along the same lines, each time the control condition is conducted, care should be taken to deliver noncontingent attention in the same exact manner.

96   Functional Analysis

Your data sheet should now look like the picture below:

[Chart: Chart Title — scatter plot with Attention, Escape, Play series, x-axis 0–14, y-axis 0–14]

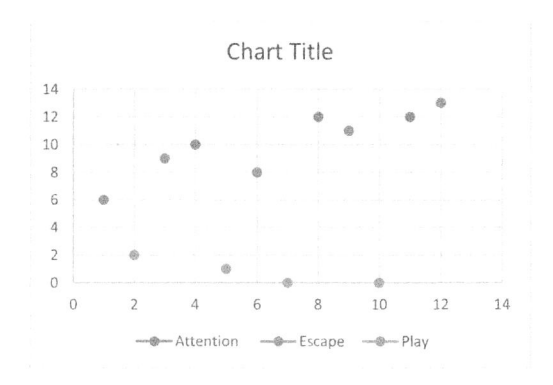

2. Click on the graph and select "Move Chart," then select "New sheet," type in "FA Multielement Graph" and click the OK button. This will move your chart to a separate sheet and make it easier to work with.

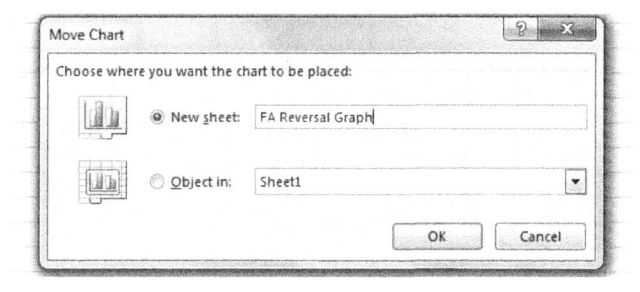

[Move Chart dialog box: New sheet: FA Reversal Graph]

Editing the Graph

1. Delete the gridlines as you did in the reversal graph, by left clicking on the lines and hitting the delete button
2. Now connect the isolated data points with a data path
    a. Left click on one of the data paths, then right click and choose "Select Data." This will bring you back to the data sheet with a new menu, and should look like the picture below

Figure 6.1 Continued.

Trend is the direction of the data path and can be described as increasing or upward, decreasing or downward, or no (or zero) trend. In the test condition, if the data are on an increasing trend that would provide at least partial evidence that the clinician has identified a relevant reinforcer for the problem behavior of study. However, if the data are on a decreasing trend, that would argue against that variable as being a relevant reinforcer. When analyzing trends within the

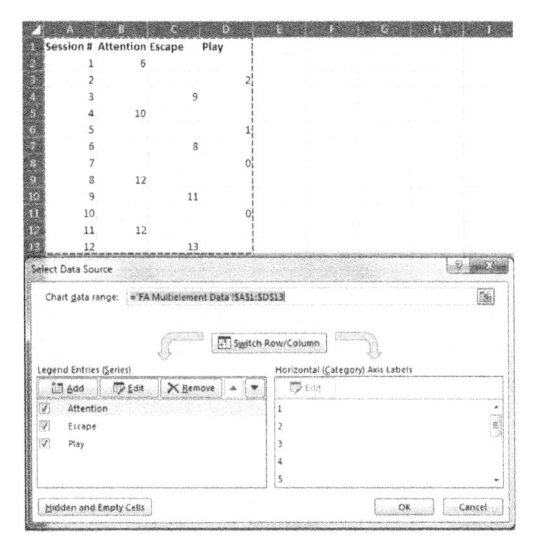

b. Click on the menu option, "Hidden and Empty Cells"
c. In the field "Show empty cells as:" select "Connect data points with line"

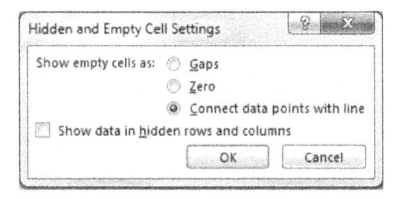

d. Your graph should now look like the picture below:

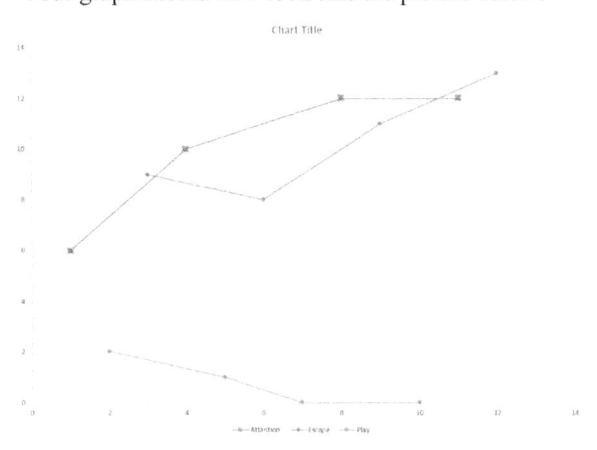

e. Next, follow the steps as you did for the reversal graph to edit the graph further (e.g., move the Legend, increase font of legend, make data paths and points black and white, eliminate borders, add axis labels, etc)
f. Once you are done, your graph should look like the one below

Figure 6.1 Continued.

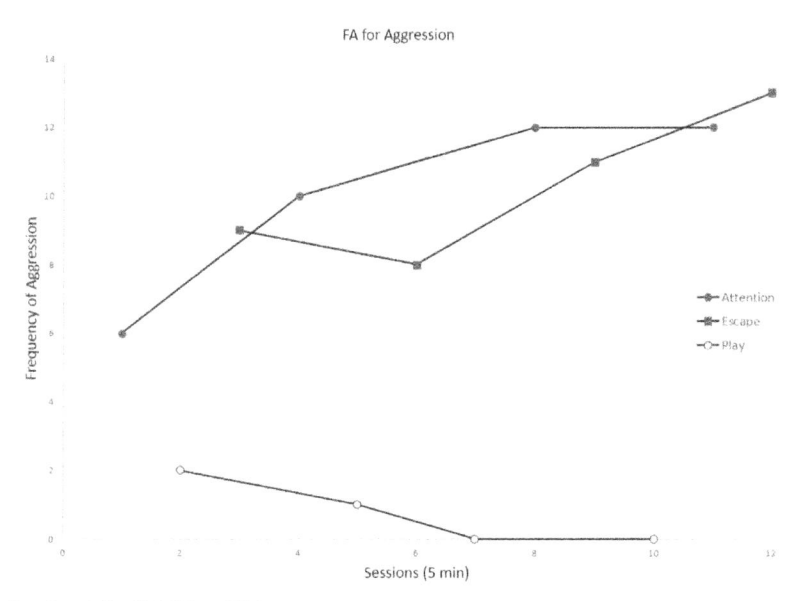

FA for Aggression

[Graph showing Frequency of Aggression vs Sessions (5 min), with three lines labeled Attention, Escape, and Play]

Bar Graph for Trial Based FAs

Creating bar graphs is quite simple and requires much less editing.

Entering Data

Enter your data in the manner displayed below:

Condition	Control	Test
Attention	5	60
Demand	10	80
Tangible	8	8

Figure 6.1 Continued.

control condition, a decreasing trend would allow greater differentiation between conditions while an increasing trend in the control condition would require further analysis.

Level is determined by evaluating where the data point values on the vertical axis converge. A mean level line can be drawn to help you determine the level of the data, but trend needs to be taken into account as well.

Baseline logic—reversal designs

Baseline logic must be considered when analyzing data within a reversal design. We use the steady-state strategy to establish a stable pattern

Creating the Graph

1. Highlight all of the cells (including labels)
2. Click on the "Insert" menu tab
3. Select "Insert Column or Bar Chart" from the Charts section
4. In the 2-D Column area, Select "Clustered Column"

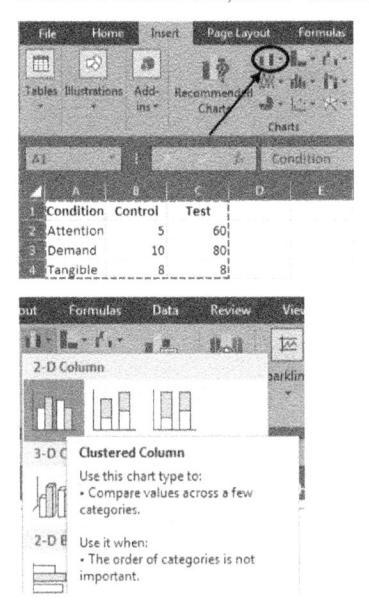

Editing the Graph

1. Move the graph to a new tab, delete the grid lines, remove the borders, and edit the graph title as you did before
2. You do not need to add an x-axis title for this type of graph; however, add a y-axis title that reads, "% of Trials with (Target Behavior)"
3. Your graph should now look like the picture below – notice that your y-axis overlaps with the numbers on the y-axis. This will need to be fixed.

Figure 6.1 Continued.

of responding so that we can draw more accurate conclusions about data that we collect during subsequent phases. The steady-state strategy entails repeatedly exposing the child or adult to a given condition while trying to eliminate or control any extraneous influences on the behavior. This allows the clinician to obtain a stable pattern of responding prior to introducing the next condition.

The three main components of baseline logic include prediction, verification, and replication. A key component of the scientific process

Trial Based FA

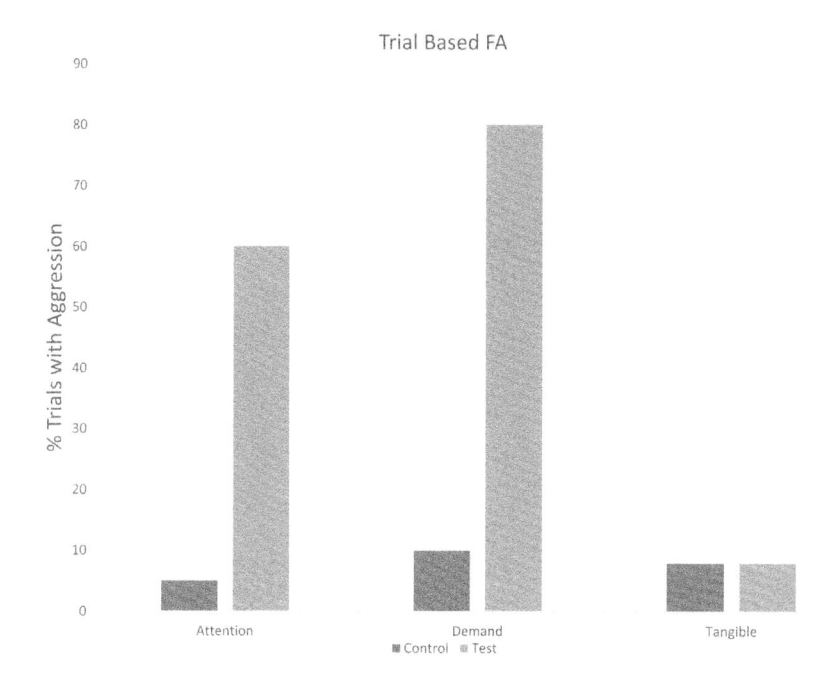

[Bar chart showing % Trials with Aggression across Attention, Demand, and Tangible conditions with Control and Test bars. Attention: Control ~5, Test ~60. Demand: Control ~10, Test ~80. Tangible: Control ~8, Test ~8.]

4. Click in the plot area to select the graph, then left click on a corner of the graph and drag it toward the center of the screen to shrink your graph and make room for the y-axis title. You can now click on the y-axis title and drag it to the left a bit to create some further separation from numbers on the y-axis.

Figure 6.1 Continued.

is the development of a hypothesis that is based on reason and observation. The hypothesis the clinician develops marks the beginning of the experiment. The clinician starts the analysis by *predicting* what he or she thinks will happen with the data. The longer the period in which stable responding is obtained, the better predictive powers of those measures. For example, if aggression in the Play condition has been at a rate of two instances per session then the next session was four instances per session, then two per session, then four per session, and that went on for month, the clinician would likely feel more confident about his or her prediction of what the data will be the next session. If the clinician is basing his or her prediction on only two sessions of data, his or her confidence about what the next data point will look like is going to much lower. This example highlights the relevance of number of data points as it relates to graph interpretation.

Graphing, graph interpretation, managing undifferentiated data   101

5. Increase the font of your legend, and drag it so it is closer to your graph. You can also re-locate the legend toward the right side border as you did in the multielement graph if you prefer. When you are done, your graph should look like the picture below:

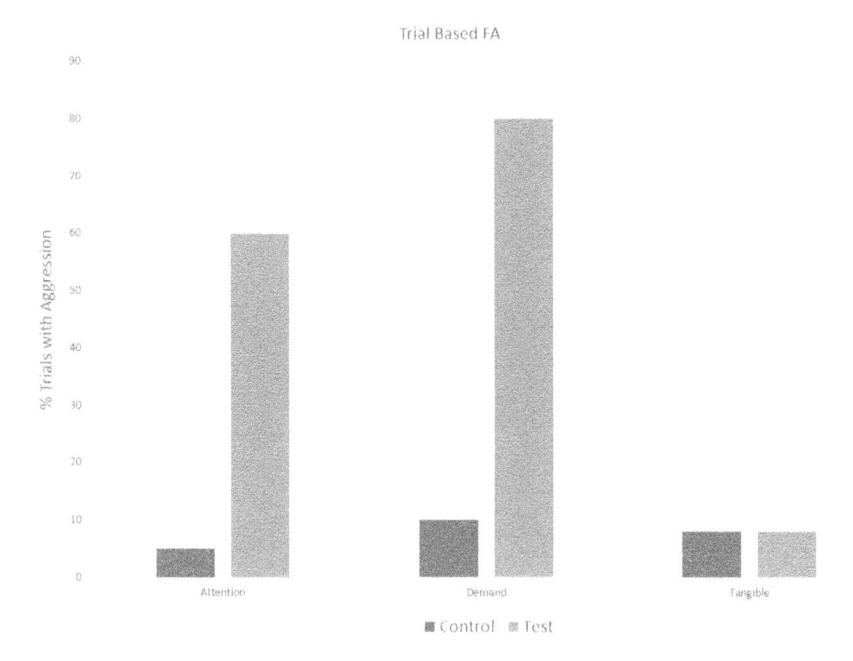

[Bar graph titled "Trial Based FA" with y-axis labeled "% Trials with Aggression" (0–90) and x-axis showing conditions: Attention, Demand, Tangible. Legend: Control, Test.]

6. Lastly, edit the color of your bars so they are black and white. We prefer to use black fill for test conditions, white fill for control conditions. Also, keep in mind, if you had an Ignore condition, both bars would be white since there is no test condition.
7. You will notice the x-axis line is faint, and the y-axis does not have a solid line
    a. Left click on the y-axis
    b. Right click, select "Format Axis"
    c. In the "Axis Options" field, choose the "Fill & Line" option
    d. Under the "Line" category, choose "Solid Line" then pick the color black

Figure 6.1 Continued.

In the Play condition, if behavior is maintained by a social function, the clinician would expect that rates of the target challenging behavior would remain low since he or she is providing frequent access to attention and tangibles, while also not introducing any demands. Therefore the clinician would predict that if he or she kept implementing the Play condition, data for the target challenging behavior would remain low and stable.

8. Your final graph should look like the picture below:

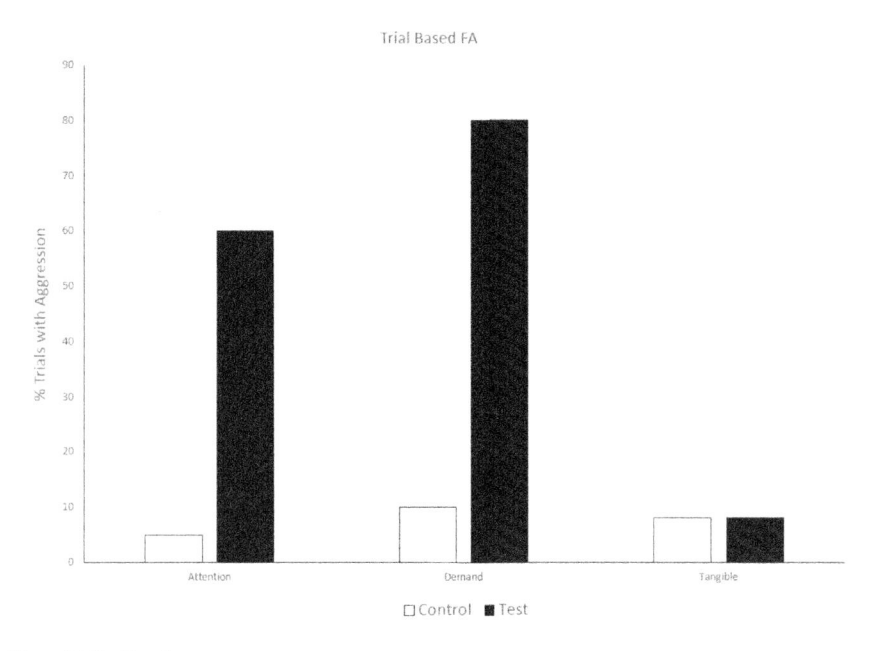

Figure 6.1 Continued.

Reversal Graph

You are measuring aggressions per 5 min FA session. Please create a reversal graph using the following data:

Session #	Data	
1	10	Attention Test
2	8	
3	12	
4	9	
5	9	
6	6	Attention Control
7	3	
8	1	
9	2	
10	1	
11	12	Attention Test
12	9	
13	11	
14	8	
15	10	
16	3	Attention Control
17	2	
18	2	
19	1	
20	1	

Figure 6.2 Graphing quiz.

Multielement Graph

You are measuring aggressions per 5 min FA session. Please create a multielement graph using the following data:

Session #	Attention	Alone	Demand	Play
1	3			
2		1		
3			8	
4				0
5	2			
6		0		
7			7	
8				1
9	0			
10		1		
11			7	
12				0
13	1			
14		0		
15			8	
16				0

Trial Based Graph

You are measuring the percentage of trials in which aggression occurred. Please create a trial-based FA graph to depict the following data:

Condition	Control	Test
Attention	15	15
Demand	20	100
Tangible	10	20

Figure 6.2 Continued.

Verification occurs when the data path remains the same in the subsequent control condition phases, after the independent variable has introduced. In other words the clinician is verifying that the data would have remained at the same level, trend, and variability in the original control phase had the clinician not introduced a new condition (e.g., Attention condition) and kept running control sessions instead. During an FA, verification can occur once the clinician has established stable responding in the Play condition (or control condition) and has

104 Functional Analysis

Reversal Design

Figure 6.3 Answer key for graphing quiz.

Multielement Design

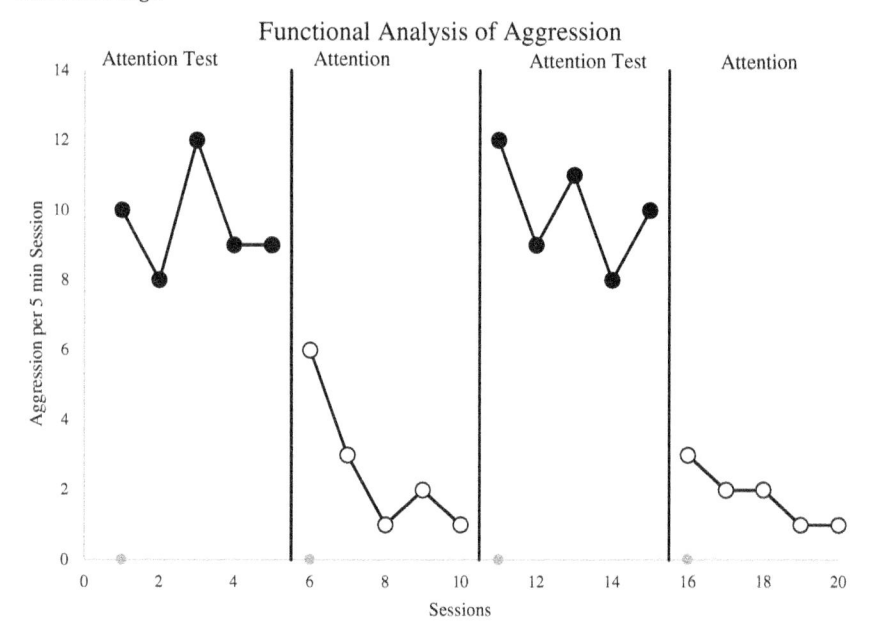

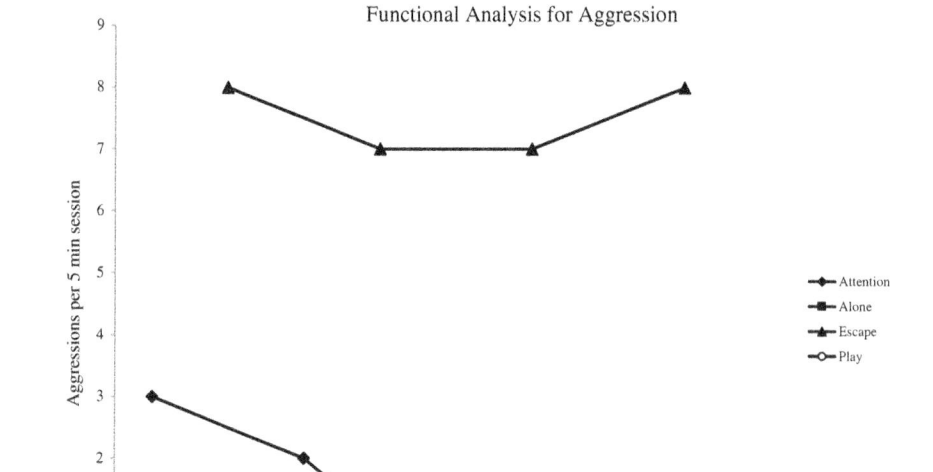

Trial-Based FA Graph

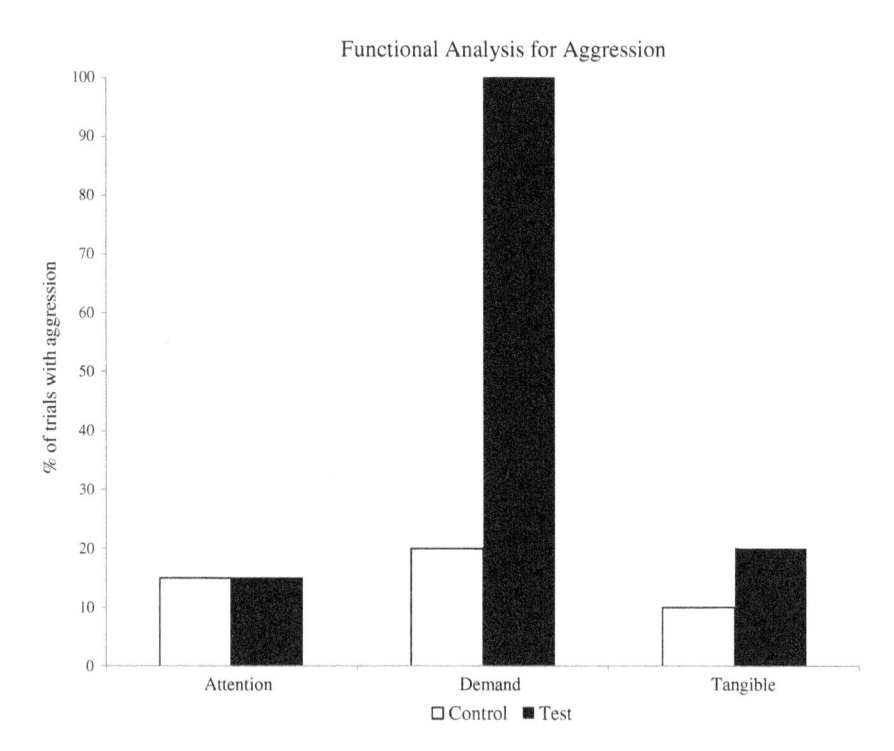

Functional Analysis for Aggression

Figure 6.3 Continued.

introduced a test condition and noticed a change in the level of the data. At this point the clinician cannot claim that the introduction of the independent variable in the test condition led to a change in the level of the data, because some other cooccurring variable may have been present at the time of the change (e.g., perhaps the child or adult became ill when the clinician switched to the test condition, which led to a more frequent display of the target behavior, such as aggression). In order to verify that the data would have remained the same had you remained in the Play (control) condition, the clinician needs to return to the Play (control) condition and observe a similar pattern of data as was observed during the previous Play (control) phase.

Replication provides further evidence that the independent variable is the relevant change in the environment that is responsible for a

Trainee: _____ Date: _____

Criterion	Points
Reversal Graph	
Correct units & range along y axis	
Correct units and range along x axis	
Correct axis label for y axis (includes length of session)	
Correct axis label for x axis	
Chart title	
Phase change lines in correct place	
Phase labels	
Lines not connected across different phases	
Data points and data paths are in black (no color)	
No border around graph	
Total Points for Graph (out of 10 pts)	

Figure 6.4 Scoring rubrics for graphing quiz.

change in behavior. For example, if data were high in the attention condition during the initial phase of the test condition, and then high again in a second phase of the test condition, the effects of that independent variable will have been replicated.

Experimental control—multielement graphs

Experimental control is measured by the degree of separation between the test and control conditions, and the predictable and

Trainee: _____   Date: _____

Criterion	Points
Multielement Graph	
Correct units & range along y axis	
Correct units and range along x axis	
Correct axis label for y axis (includes length of session)	
Correct axis label for x axis	
Chart title	
Data points and data paths are in black (no color)	
No border around graph	
Legend present	
Markers are different for each condition	
All four conditions represented with correct data values	
Total Points for Graph (out of 10 pts)	

Figure 6.4 Continued.

reliable differences between them. The more the data overlap, the less able the clinician is to draw conclusions that an independent variable led to a change in the rate of behavior. When there is little overlap between a control and test condition and the clinician observes stable levels or opposing trends, a clear demonstration of experimental control exists.

Trainee: _____   Date: _____

Criterion	Points
Trial-Based Graph	
Correct units & range along y axis (0 – 100)	
Correct axis label for y axis (percentage of trials w/ aggression)	
Correct axis labels for x axis (attention, demand, tangible)	
Chart title	
Bar graphs are in black (no color)	
No border around graph	
Legend present	
Bar patterns are different across test and control conditions	
All three conditions represented with correct data values	
Total Points for Graph (out of 9 pts)	

Figure 6.4 Continued.

If overlap exists, a degree of experimental control can be demonstrated if at least the majority of data points for a test condition fall outside of the range of values for the control condition. When one or more test conditions can be distinguished from the control condition, multiple functions for the problem behavior have been established. If the control condition is the highest or significantly overlaps with your test conditions, the data are undifferentiated—it may be that the behavior is maintained by automatic reinforcement.

6.5 Reproducible figures for graph interpretation

Name: _____   Date: _____

Please write in the function (s) for each graph or if the function is unclear, write "undifferentiated."

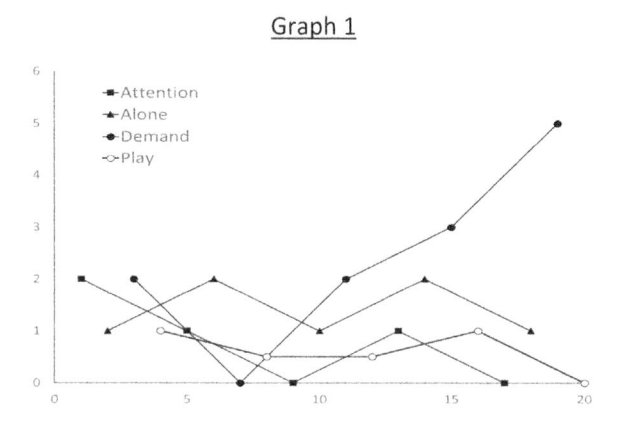

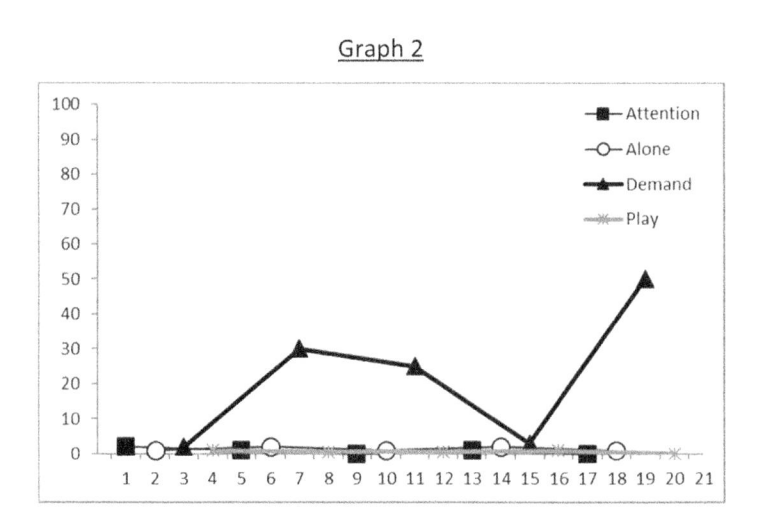

Graph 1

Graph 2

Figure 6.5 Graph interpretation quiz.

Graph 3

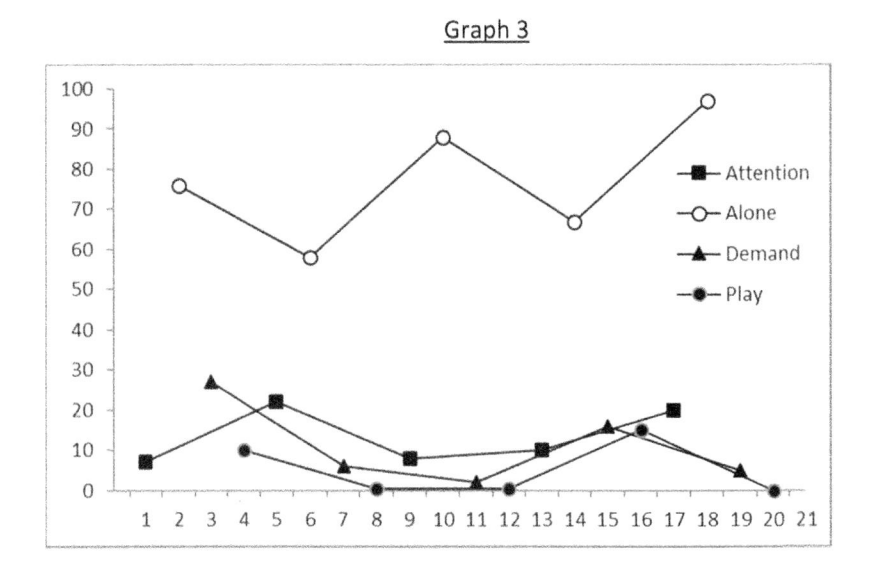

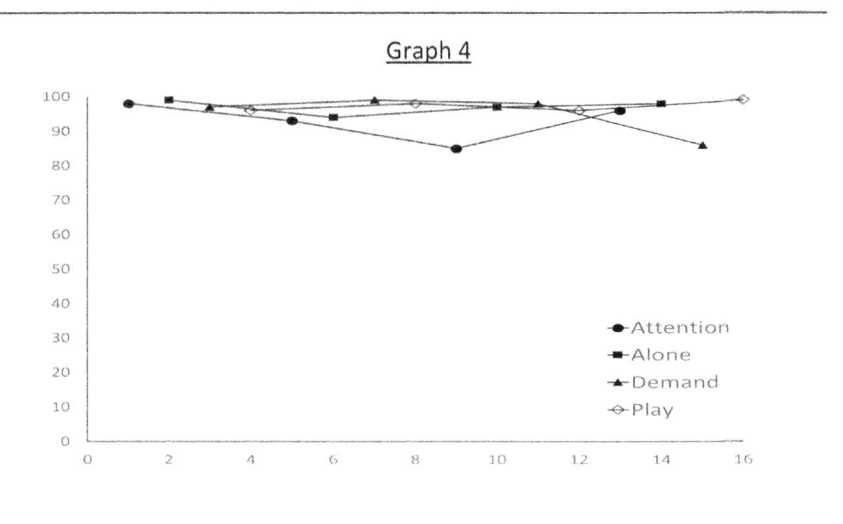

Graph 4

Figure 6.5 Continued.

6.6 Managing undifferentiated data

When determining how to manage undifferentiated FA data, consider whether the data are high and undifferentiated, or if the data are low and undifferentiated. If the data are high and undifferentiated then this

Graphing, graph interpretation, managing undifferentiated data   111

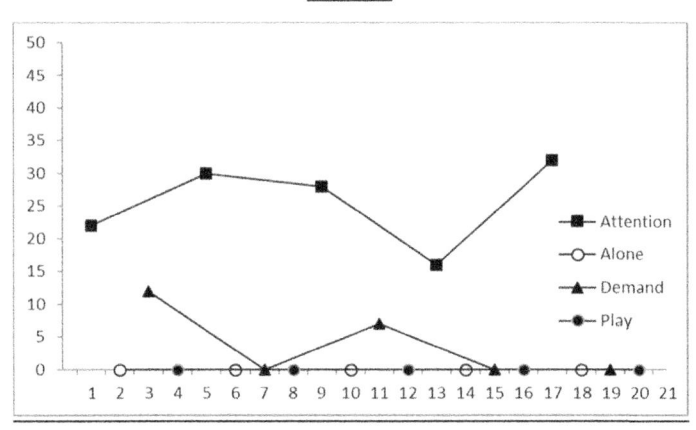

Graph 5

Graph 6

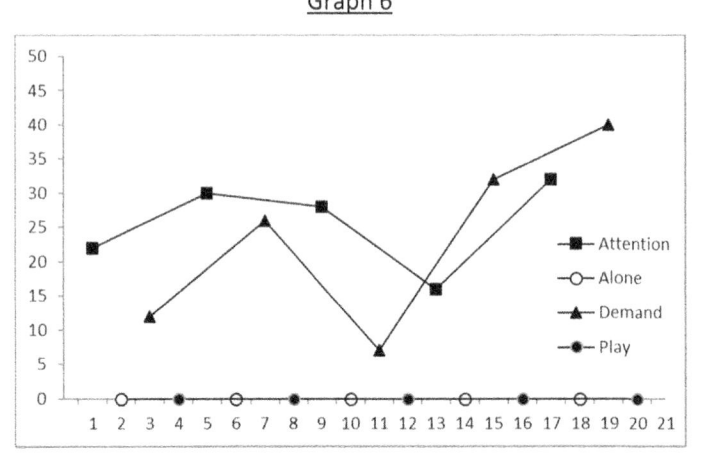

Figure 6.5 Continued.

means that despite the environmental changes made between conditions, behavior continues to occur at a high rate. There are several reasons why this may be happening.

112 Functional Analysis

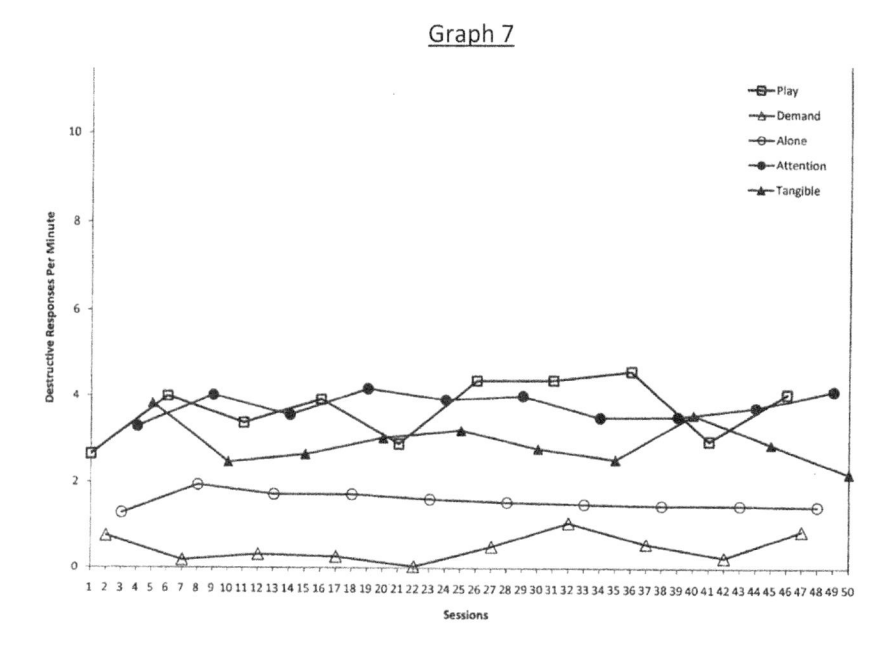

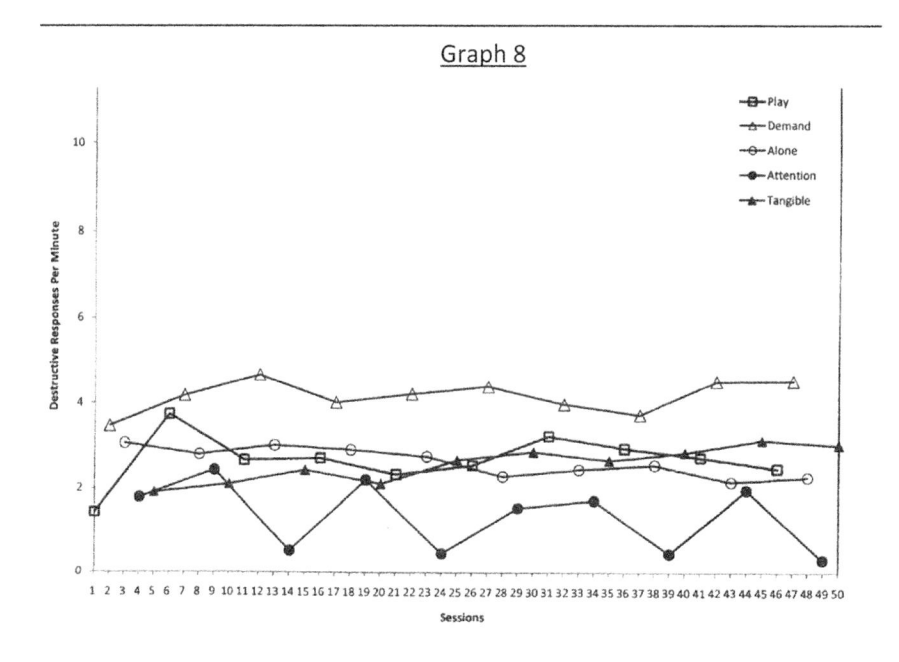

Graph 7

Graph 8

Figure 6.5 Continued.

Graph 9

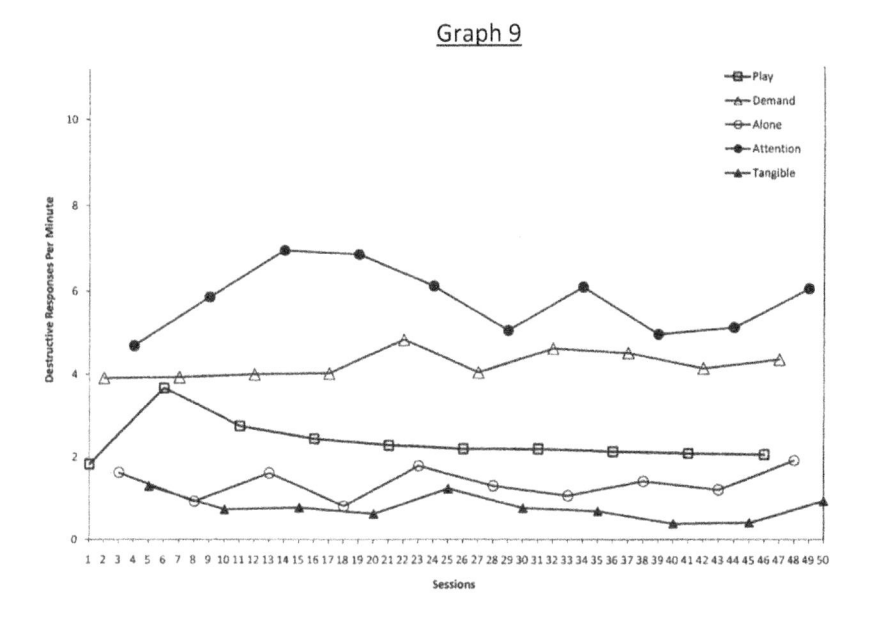

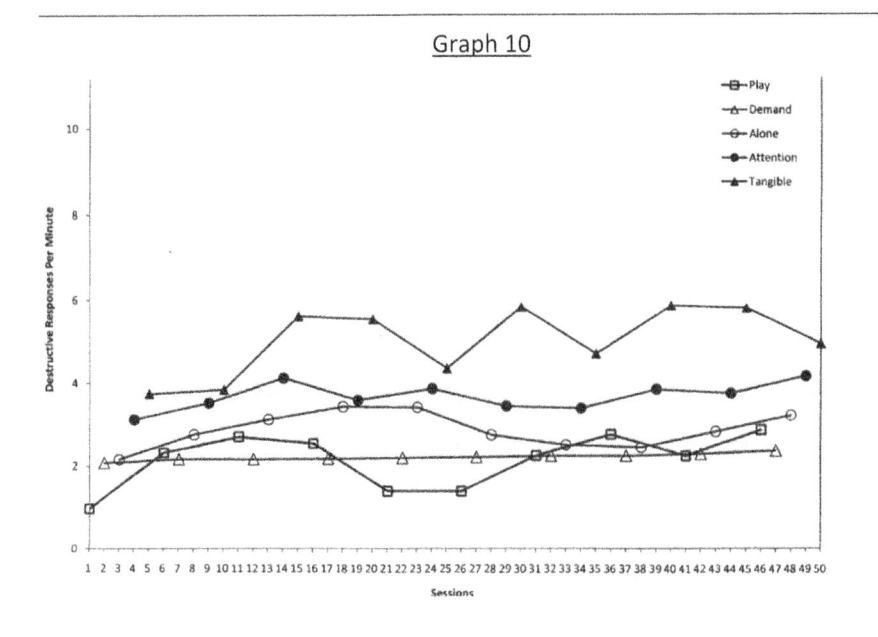

Graph 10

Figure 6.5 Continued.

1) Escape

2) Escape

3) Automatic

4) Undifferentiated (Automatic)

5) Attention

6) Escape, Attention

7) Undifferentiated (Automatic)

8) Escape

9) Attention, Escape

10) Tangible, Attention

Figure 6.6 Answer key graph interpretation quiz.

Failure to discriminate between conditions

It is possible that a child or adult undergoing assessment has not been able to discriminate when new contingencies or environmental changes have gone into effect. For example, consider the attention and play conditions. In both conditions a child is presented with toys. If problem behavior occurred at a high rate in the attention condition, the clinician would have been providing a good amount of contingent praise in the form of verbal statements and physical contact. If this condition were to be followed by a Play condition, where a similar amount of verbal and physical praise is occurring as well, the conditions may appear to be no different to the child.

Carryover effects

Carryover effects may also be occurring across conditions. For example a child or adult may not display problem for the first 2 minutes of the attention condition. However, in the last 2 minutes the target behavior, self-injurious behavior (SIB), begins to occur, and the rate increases over time. The child or adult may exhibit a high degree of emotional responding, perhaps even throwing or destroying objects. The clinician then ends the session and begins a tangible condition. The child or adult throws the objects again and begins engaging in SIB. It is possible that given the degree of distress the client experienced in the attention condition, it is now carrying over to the tangible condition and influencing the rate of SIB in that condition.

Automatic reinforcement

Another possibility is that the social contingencies the clinician is manipulating have no influence on the rate of behavior. For example, consider stereotypic behavior, such as repetitive speech, that is maintained by automatic reinforcement. No matter what social elements the clinician adjusts across conditions, this behavior will still likely occur as the behavior itself is producing the reinforcer. Let's take a moment to consider how you can adjust your assessment should you encounter each of these situations.

Addressing challenges with discrimination

If the child or adult is having a difficult time discriminating between conditions, the clinician can build in salient stimuli that are associated with each condition. For example the clinician might wear a different colored or patterned shirt unique to each condition, or wear a hat or jacket on in one condition, but not another. The clinician might also use different therapists for each condition, although he or she would need to make sure that there is not a variable associated with a particular person that could influence responding (e.g., problem behavior tends to be evoked by larger males).

Addressing carryover effects

In terms of carryover effects, it may be helpful to conduct a within-session analysis. This can be done by dividing session data into smaller bins of time and graphing occurrences by bin. For example, consider the scenario described earlier, in which the clinician notices an increase in responding toward the end of the attention session. When analyzing the data in the subsequent tangible condition, it may be that the rate of problem behavior started out high (the carryover), but then diminished as the session continued. If you were to graph behavior for the each of these whole sessions, the rates may be equivalent. However, when you look at your data using a within-session analysis, you may identify this pattern and determine that a carryover effect is occurring across these adjacent conditions.

If such a pattern were evident, one option would be to build in longer breaks between sessions so that the client has the opportunity to settle down. Clear discriminative stimuli across conditions, which was mentioned as a solution for children or adults who are having difficulty discriminating between conditions, can also be helpful in this circumstance. Perhaps a child or adult has become agitated in a social avoidance condition which could carry over into an ignore condition. A clear signal that attention is about to be removed (if attention is aversive) could lead to a reduction in behavior.

Another option is to change the experimental design. Rapid alternation between conditions may contribute to both carryover effects and discrimination challenges, so utilizing a reversal design could be helpful. Such a design would allow the child or adult to experience the same contingency over and over again. Since there is less switching between conditions, there is less of an opportunity for carryover effects.

Addressing potential automatic reinforcement

If you hypothesize that problem behavior is not influenced by social contingencies, it is worth considering conducting an extended alone/ignore session. This involves running either one long alone/ignore session (e.g., 30 minutes) or running shorter alone/ignore sessions back-to-back. If problem behavior is maintained by automatic reinforcement, you would expect high rates of behavior to persist absent of social contingencies. If it does, you have evidence for an automatic reinforcement function.

If behavior declines during the extended alone condition, particularly if it drops to zero, it may be that problem behavior is socially mediated, but there is another issue, such as those described previously, influencing behavior. You should keep in mind, however, that behavior could decline in an extended alone/ignore session as a result of satiation to the automatic reinforcer. This will be something you will need to evaluate when determining next steps (e.g., do you want to repeat the extended alone session the following day, or shorten its length to 15 minutes, then conduct sessions in a more spaced manner?).

Addressing low and undifferentiated data

There may be times when you conduct an FA in which the target behavior does not occur, or occurs at a very low frequency. If your data are low/zero and undifferentiated then you are having trouble evoking problem behavior. If you cannot evoke problem behavior then you are not going to be able to determine a function. If this occurs, you will need to consider what variables are currently absent from your assessment that could be relevant. It would probably be a good idea to conduct additional interviews with people who know the client well, as well as observe the client in the natural environment, perhaps when others predict problem behavior will be more likely.

Gathering additional information

The information you will want to gather includes learning more about the establishing operations that enhance the value of the reinforcer. For example, what makes escape more or less valuable? Could it be the pace of instruction, loud noise in the environment while instruction is being delivered, or a particular type of task (e.g., instruction while seated vs gross motor exercises)?

You may also consider what discriminative stimuli could be included in your assessment to signal the availability of reinforcement, or what *s*-deltas could be removed. For example, perhaps a child or adult wears a helmet each time they get up from their desk to transition to a new environment given the fall risk associated with ambulating. The event of the staff member picking up the helmet off a shelf could signal to the child or adult that a transition will be occurring. If problem behavior, such as SIB, is maintained by escape from transitions, the child or adult may begin engaging in SIB when the staff member picks up the helmet. If this were to be the case, incorporating the helmet into the assessment would be helpful. It is also possible that a particular teacher or caregiver may signal availability of reinforcement, so you could arrange to have that person be a therapist.

It is also important to consider that there may be a stimulus in your assessment that is suppressing responding. For example, perhaps you are video recording sessions and a camera operator is in the room with

118   Functional Analysis

the therapist. The problem behavior may have been previously extinguished in the presence of multiple staff, and therefore it is suppressed in this condition. In this scenario, setting up a camera that can be operated remotely would allow a single staff member to be in the room, which could then serve as a discriminative stimulus that reinforcement is available for problem behavior and lead to its occurrence during that condition.

6.7 Reproducible figures for managing undifferentiated data

Name: _____   Date: _____

1) What are three possible reasons for FA data that are high and undifferentiated (3 pts)?

2) You have just conducted a few 5 min sessions of a standard functional analysis and you are concerned that responding during one condition (e.g., the attention condition) is influencing responding in the next condition (e.g., the play condition). You decide to conduct a within-session analysis.

   How would you do this (1 pt)?

   What pattern of responding across the two conditions would provide evidence for your hypothesis (2 pts)?

3) When using a multi-element design, you determine that responding in one condition is contaminating responding in other conditions. What change could you make to your existing FA to reduce this possibility? What change in experimental design might you make and why might this help?

   Change to existing FA (1 pt):

Figure 6.7 Managing undifferentiated data quiz.

Change in experimental design and why (2 pts):

4) Following a functional analysis in which the data were high and undifferentiated across multiple experimental conditions, you hypothesize that the student's target behavior may be maintained by automatic reinforcement.

What could you do to further explore this possibility (1 pt)?

What pattern of data would support your hypothesis (1 pt)?

What pattern of data would provide evidence against your hypothesis (1 pt)?

5) You recently conducted a functional analysis and the target behavior did not occur across conditions. What should you do next (name at least two steps)?

Step 1 (1 pt):

Step 2 (1 pt):

Total Points (out of 14 pts): _____

Figure 6.7 Continued.

Name: _____ Date: _____

1) What are three possible reasons for FA data that are high and undifferentiated (3 pts)?
   1. *Difficulty discriminating between conditions*
   2. *Carryover effects*
   3. *Behavior is maintained by automatic reinforcement*

2) You have just conducted a few 5 min sessions of a standard functional analysis and you are concerned that responding during one condition (e.g., the attention condition) is influencing responding in the next condition (e.g., the play condition). You decide to conduct a within-session analysis.

   How would you do this (1 pt)?

   Break the 5 min session into smaller bins of time (e.g., 30 sec) and graph data for each of those bins to determine if there are within-session patterns of your data

   What pattern of responding across the two conditions would provide evidence for your hypothesis (2 pts)?

   - *An escalating rate of responding, or high and stable responding, in the attention condition*
   - *Higher rates of responding during the initial part of the play condition, then a decreasing trend of behavior as the play session continued*

3) When using a multielement design, you determine responding in one condition is contaminating responding in other conditions. What change could you make to your existing FA to reduce this possibility? What change in experimental design might you make and why might this help?

   Change to existing FA (1 pt):

   Either one of the following:
   - *You could build in more time between conditions OR*
   - *Correlate more salient stimuli to signal changes between conditions*

Figure 6.8 Answer key for managing undifferentiated data quiz.

Change in experimental design and why (2 pts):

You could change from a multielement design to a reversal design.

Doing so allows the individual to experience more consecutive instances of the response–reinforcer relationship, and when you change conditions, contamination should be highest at the beginning of the new phase, with more time for behavior to diminish as consecutive sessions of the new condition are conducted. Eliminating rapid alternation of conditions may also facilitate discrimination between conditions.

4) Following a functional analysis in which the data were high and undifferentiated across multiple experimental conditions, you hypothesize that the student's target behavior may be maintained by automatic reinforcement.

What could you do to further explore this possibility (1 pt)?

Conduct an extended alone/ignore condition

What pattern of data would support your hypothesis (1 pt)?

Continued high rates of the challenging behavior

What pattern of data would provide evidence against your hypothesis (1 pt)?

A decline in challenging behavior, especially if the behavior reduces to zero rates (although it is still possible the individual may have become satiated following repeated unrestricted access to the reinforcer)

Figure 6.8 Continued.

5) You recently conducted a functional analysis and the target behavior did not occur across conditions. What should you do next (name at least two steps)?

Step 1 (1 pt):

Follow-up steps to gather more relevant information:

- *Interview staff members again, conduct further observation of the individual with the goal of identifying other variables that might evoke/elicit problem behavior*
- *Identify relevant EOs that were absent or weak in your first FA*
- *Identify S^d s that were absent/not very salient that signal availability of reinforcement*
- *Identify potential S^p s that were either present and leading to a suppression of problem behavior, or absent, and if present, would signal punishment and lead to an increase in behavior maintained by escape*

Step 2 (1 pt):

Incorporate the new information you gathered into your FA:

- *Build in the relevant variables described above into a new FA*
- *Remove any stimuli that may be suppressing responding*
- *You could also extend FA sessions to allow the EO to build over time, or wait for problem behavior to occur and then initiate FA sessions*

Total Possible Points = 14 pts

Figure 6.8 Continued.

CHAPTER 7

Supervision and mentoring

7.1 Overview of training procedures

At this final level of the functional analysis (FA) training curriculum, trainers supervise trainees implementing FA sessions with children and adults. The objective is to confirm that trainees are competent conducting each of the FA methodologies they were taught, independently, and under natural conditions within educational and treatment settings. Upon completion, a certificate can be presented to trainees to signify that they have successfully qualified all levels of the FA training curriculum and are able to design and implement FA sessions proficiently. Unlike prior levels, Level 7 of the FA training curriculum does not include presentation slides and relies on in vivo supervision by the trainer.

Trainees begin at the preanalysis phase by identifying a child or adult in their setting to participate in FA. With support from the trainer, they complete the *planning portfolio for conducting a functional analysis* shown in Fig. 7.1. This document focuses trainees on several key requirements for creating their FA, namely, preassessment preparation, ethical considerations, methodology, experimental design, measurement, and scheduling sessions. Trainees complete the planning portfolio independently, with subsequent feedback from the trainer. As well, we recommend that trainees present their planning protocols within group meetings among the trainer, clinicians, and therapists. In addition to supervision from the trainer, the group format provides further feedback to trainees about their planned FA, suggested revisions, and steps toward creating a final product.

Once the trainer approves the planning portfolio, the trainee conducts the FA with accompanying therapists as dictated by the methodology with each child or adult. The trainer should be present during all FA sessions in order to supervise procedures, discuss pertinent issues, and resolve any unanticipated outcomes. The trainer interacts with the trainee in vivo following each condition of the FA and uses the same performance feedback methods that were applied throughout the FA training curriculum. That is, the trainer reviews the correspondence between planned and actual procedures, reinforces the trainee's implementation integrity, and corrects errors, as warranted.

The trainee documents FA results on the *postanalysis training form* (Fig. 7.2), starting with a graph that accurately conforms to the experimental design. Based on the graphic depiction, the trainee is requested to interpret the findings and consider applicable options. For example, are the data from the FA sufficient to determine behavior function or are additional analyses indicated because the data were undifferentiated? In the case of conclusive FA results, what hypotheses will the trainee formulate to inform decisions about intervention? Typically, supervision at this level focuses principally on the trainee's data-evaluation and critical thinking abilities.

The trainer completes the *portfolio scoring sheet* presented in Fig. 7.3 to record trainee performance at the preanalysis and postanalysis phases. The sheet lists individual training components and a dichotomous scoring rubric (yes–no) that documents "Did the trainee sufficiently address the component of training?" A trainee passes the final level of the FA training curriculum when her/his overall "yes" score is 90% or higher. If a trainee scores less than 90%, additional training is provided on those components that received "no" ratings, followed by reevaluation to ensure that performance reaches the 90% or greater criterion.

Upon satisfactory completion of the FA training curriculum, trainees continue to receive supervision designing, implementing, and interpreting FA sessions. For example, in our human services organization, former trainees assume FA responsibilities within program teams comprising senior clinicians who routinely monitor their performance through observation, feedback, and mentoring. We have found that integrating former trainees in this way ensures built-in support and direction for them mastering and refining FA skills under real-world clinical conditions with children and adults.

Throughout the final level of the FA training curriculum, we advise trainers to supervise trainees in line with procedures and guidelines that are considered best practices and have emerging evidence support (Sellers, Alai-Rosales, & MacDonald, 2016; Sellers, Valentino, &

LeBlanc, 2016; Turner, 2017; Turner, Fischer, & Luiselli, 2016; Valentino, LeBlanc, & Sellers, 2016). Specifically, supervision should be aligned with the unique and individually determined training and performance needs of each trainee with emphasis on:

1. directly observing trainees when implementing FA;
2. delivering behavior-contingent performance feedback through positive reinforcement and correction; and
3. evaluating implementation integrity according to behaviorally anchored written checklists.

We suggest that supervision will be most effective when trainers socially validate their interactions and training methods with trainees, specifically their satisfaction and approval of training objectives, procedures, and outcomes. And as described throughout this guidebook, supervision of trainees designing and implementing FA must consider matters of culture and diversity, the resources available at educational and treatment settings, and the prevailing ethical codes of practice.

Finally, trainers must be sure that they have adequate time for supervising trainees as they acquire the competencies necessary for conducting FA sessions independently. Supervising caseloads should not be so burdensome that requisite observations of and performance feedback to trainees are compromised. Also, for some trainees, the frequency and duration of trainer supervision may have to be increased in order to achieve optimal results. Accordingly, trainers should adapt their schedules so that time is available when the need for additional supervision arises.

Training steps for Level 6
1. Trainer instructs trainee in completing *planning portfolio for conducting a functional analysis*.
2. Trainer supervises trainee implementing FA.
3. Trainer documents FA results on *postanalysis training form*.
4. Trainer completes *portfolio scoring sheet*.
5. Posttraining supervision continues with trainee.

Criteria to pass Level 6
Score of 90% or higher on *portfolio scoring sheet*

126 Functional Analysis

7.2 Reproducible figures and forms

Trainee Name: _____   Trainer's Name: _____

Client Name: _____   Target Behavior: _____

Date: _____

Operational Definition of Target Behavior:
_____
_____
_____
_____

Pre-Assessment

1. Which form will you use to guide your interview?

   _____

2. Who will you interview during the pre-assessment?

Name	Role

Figure 7.1 Planning portfolio for conducting a functional analysis.

3. Will you use any other information to inform your pre-assessment (e.g., descriptive analysis, previous FA results)? If so, please describe below, if not write "N/A"

4. What antecedent conditions did you identify that may evoke the target behavior?

5. What S^Ds or establishing operations did you identify that either signal the availability of reinforcement for challenging behavior or increase the likelihood of the challenging behavior given the increased value of the reinforcer?

   S^Ds:

   Establishing operations:

6. What consequences do you hypothesize are maintaining challenging behavior?

Figure 7.1 Continued.

Ethical Considerations

Please list ethical concerns you have considered based upon your pre-assessment. What safeguards will you incorporate into your FA to minimize any harm or discomfort the student might experience?

Safety Risks Associated with the Proposed Assessment:

1. _____
2. _____
3. _____

Ethical Concerns:

1. _____
2. _____
3. _____

Safeguards:

1. _____
2. _____
3. _____

Methodology

Based upon the information gathered in your interviews and your observation of the student, what FA methodology have you chosen? What is the rationale for your choice?

Methodology: _____

Rationale:

Figure 7.1 Continued.

_____
_____
_____

Experimental Design

What experimental design have you chosen? What influenced your decision?

Design: _____

Rationale:

_____
_____
_____
_____

Measurement

What measurement system have you chosen? Why do you think this is the best system for your FA (please attach data sheet)?

Measurement: _____

Rationale:

_____
_____
_____

Schedule of Conducting Functional Analysis

After your planning form is approved, In the area below, identify dates and times over the next two weeks that you are available to conduct functional analysis sessions. Please provide at least 48 hours notice to your mentor and ensure he or she is available to observe the sessions prior to finalizing the schedule. The goal is to be able to conduct a functional analysis within an efficient time frame.

Date	Time	Date	Time

Figure 7.1 Continued.

_____
_____
_____
_____

_____   _____
Signature of Trainee   Signature of Trainer

Figure 7.1 Continued.

Trainee Name: _____   Trainer Name: _____

Client Name: _____   Target Behavior: _____

Date: _____

Graphing

Please display the graph(s) from your functional analysis below:

Based upon the results depicted in your graph, can you determine a function, and if so what is the hypothesized function(s) for the target behavior?

_____

If your data were undifferentiated, what next steps will you take (when you conduct a new FA, please complete this form again)?

Figure 7.2 Postanalysis reporting form.

Given these results, what intervention do you propose to address the target behavior and functional, alternative response? Include the name of the procedure, a technological description of the exact procedures to be followed in its implementation, and explain how the procedures are conceptually systematic. Please do this for all elements of the treatment plan.

Signature of Trainee   Signature of Trainer

Figure 7.2 Continued.

132   Functional Analysis

Trainee Name: _____   Supervisor's Name: _____

Client Name: _____   Target Behavior: _____

Date: _____

Training Component	Did the Trainee Sufficiently Address the Component of Training?	Comments
Interview Process		
Trainee selects an appropriate interview form and interviews relevant staff members/caregivers	Yes No	
Identified antecedent conditions that precede target behavior	Yes No	
Identified relevant S^Ds	Yes No	
Identified relevant establishing operations	Yes No	
Consequences described are consistent with the identified antecedent conditions, S^Ds, and	Yes No	

Figure 7.3 Portfolio scoring sheet.

establish operations		
Ethical Considerations		
Inquired about and determined the potential safety risks associated with the target behavior	Yes No	
Ethical concerns adequately described	Yes No	
Adequately described safeguard(s) for student	Yes No	
Methodology		
Does the methodology chosen by the trainee make sense given the information obtained during the interview?	Yes No	
Does the rationale for choosing the methodology make sense?	Yes No	
Experimental Design		
Does the experimental design chosen by the trainee make sense given the information obtained during the interview?	Yes No	

Figure 7.3 Continued.

Does the rationale for choosing the experimental design make sense?	Yes No	
Measurement		
Does the measurement system chosen by the trainee make sense given the information obtained during the interview?	Yes No	
Does the rationale for choosing the measurement system make sense?	Yes No	
Graphing		
Axes on graph(s) are accurately labeled	Yes No	
Phase labels or a legend is present	Yes No	

Figure 7.3 Continued.

Appropriate graphing conventions followed: • Reversal design includes phase change lines, and data path does not cross it • Multielement design includes different markers for each FA condition • Trial-based graph has bar patterns that are different across test and control conditions	Yes No	
Interpreting Graphs		
Did the trainee identify the correct function(s) based upon the data in the graph or accurately conclude the data are undifferentiated?	Yes No	
If data were undifferentiated, the trainee correctly identified follow-up steps	Yes No N/A	
Intervention		
The intervention described matches the function(s) identified in the FA	Yes No	
The intervention described by the trainee includes appropriate steps to reduce the target behavior	Yes No	
The intervention described by the trainee includes appropriate steps to increase a functional	Yes No	

Figure 7.3 Continued.

alternative behavior		
The intervention described is technological (all contingencies well-described, all steps of the intervention clearly delineated)	Yes No	
The intervention described is conceptually systematic (it is linked to the principles and procedures of applied behavior analysis)	Yes No	

Scoring: Count up all "Yes" responses and divide by 23 (if data are not undifferentiated) or 24 (if data are undifferentiated). The number of criteria is one unit higher for undifferentiated data sets as the trainee needs to describe how they managed these data.

Overall score (must be > 90% to pass): _____

_____   _____
Signature of Trainee   Signature of Trainer

Figure 7.3 Continued.

REFERENCES

Allen, K. A., Hart, B., Buell, J. S., Harris, F. R., & Wolf, M. M. (1964). Effects of social reinforcement on isolate behavior of a nursery school child. *Child Development, 35*, 511–518.

Barlow, D. H., Nock, M. K., & Hersen, M. (2009). *Single case experimental designs: Strategies for studying behavior change* (3rd ed.). Boston, MA: Allyn and Bacon.

Beavers, G. A., & Iwata, B. A. (2011). Prevalence of multiply controlled problem behavior. *Journal of Applied Behavior Analysis, 44*, 593–597.

Beavers, G. A., Iwata, B. A., & Lerman, D. C. (2013). Thirty years of research on the functional analysis of problem behavior. *Journal of Applied Behavior Analysis, 46*, 1–21.

Behavior Analyst Certification Board. (2019). *Professional and ethics compliance code for behavior analysts*. Littleton, CO: Behavior Analyst Certification Board.

Bijou, S. W., Peterson, R. F., & Ault, M. H. (1968). A method to integrate descriptive and experimental field studies at the level of data and empirical concepts. *Journal of Applied Behavior Analysis, 1*, 175–191.

Bloom, S. E., Iwata, B. A., Fritz, J. N., Roscoe, E. M., & Carreau, A. B. (2011). Classroom application of a trial-based functional analysis. *Journal of Applied Behavior Analysis, 44*(1), 19–31.

Carr, E. G. (1977). The motivation of self-injurious behavior: A review of some hypotheses. *Psychological Bulletin, 84*, 800–816.

Chok, J. T., Shlesinger, A., Studer, L., & Bird, F. L. (2012). Description of a practitioner training program on functional analysis and treatment development. *Behavior Analysis in Practice, 5*(2), 25–36.

Cooper, J. O., Heron, T. E., & Heward, W. L. (2007). *Applied behavior analysis* (2nd ed.). Upper Saddle River, NJ: Merrill Prentice Hall.

Fahmie, T. A., Iwata, B. A., Harper, J. M., & Querim, A. C. (2013). Evaluation of the divided attention condition during functional analyses. *Journal of Applied Behavior Analysis, 46*(1), 71–78.

Fahmie, T. A., Iwata, B. A., Querim, A. C., & Harper, J. M. (2013). Test-specific control conditions for functional analyses. *Journal of Applied Behavior Analysis, 46*(1), 61–70.

Gast, D. L., & Leford, J. R. (2014). *Single case research methodology: Applications in special education and behavioral sciences*. New York: Routledge.

Hagopian, L. P., Fisher, W. W., Thompson, R. H., Owen-DeSchryver, J., Iwata, B. A., & Wacker, D. P. (1997). Toward the development of structured criteria for interpretation of functional analysis data. *Journal of Applied Behavior Analysis, 30*, 313–326.

Hanley, G. P. (2012). Functional assessment of problem behavior: Dispelling myths, overcoming implementation obstacles, and developing new lore. *Behavior Analysis in Practice, 5*(1), 54–72.

Hanley, G. P., Iwata, B. A., & McCord, B. E. (2003). Functional analysis of problem behavior: A review. *Journal of Applied Behavior Analysis, 36*(2), 147–185.

Hanley, G. P., Jin, C. S., Vanselow, N. R., & Hanratty, L. A. (2014). Producing meaningful improvements in problem behavior of children with autism via synthesized analyses and treatments. *Journal of Applied Behavior Analysis, 47*(1), 16–36.

Harper, J. M., Iwata, B. A., & Camp, E. M. (2013). Assessment and treatment of social avoidance. *Journal of Applied Behavior Analysis, 46*(1), 147–160.

Iwata, B. A., Dorsey, M. F., Slifer, K. J., Bauman, K. E., & Richman, G. S. (1994). Toward a functional analysis of self-injury. *Journal of Applied Behavior Analysis, 27*, 197–209. (Reprinted from *Analysis and Intervention in Developmental Disabilities, 2*, 3–20, 1982.).

Iwata, B. A., & Dozier, C. L. (2008). Clinical application of functional analysis methodology. *Behavior Analysis in Practice, 1*, 3–9.

Iwata, B. A., Pace, G. M., Dorsey, M. F., Zarcone, J. R., Vollmer, T. R., Smith, R. G., ... Willis, K. D. (1994). The functions of self-injurious behavior: An experimental-epidemiological analysis. *Journal of Applied Behavior Analysis, 27*, 215–240. Available from https://doi.org/10.1901/jaba.1994.27-215.

Iwata, B. A., Pace, G. M., Kalsher, M. J., Cowdery, G. E., & Cataldo, M. F. (1990). Experimental analysis and extinction of self-injurious behavior. *Journal of Applied Behavior Analysis, 23*, 11–27.

Jessel, J., Hanley, G. P., & Ghaemmaghami, M. (2016). Interview-informed synthesized contingency analyses: Thirty replications and reanalysis. *Journal of Applied Behavior Analysis, 49*, 576–595.

Kodak, T., Northup, J., & Kelley, M. E. (2007). An evaluation of the types of attention that maintain problem behavior. *Journal of Applied Behavior Analysis, 40*(1), 167–171.

Lovaas, O. I., & Simmons, J. Q. (1969). Manipulation of self-destruction in three retarded children. *Journal of Applied Behavior Analysis, 2*, 143–157.

Lydon, S., Healy, O., O'Reilly, M. F., & Lang, R. (2012). Variations in functional analysis methodology: A systematic review. *Journal of Developmental and Physical Disabilities, 24*(3), 301–326.

Mace, F. C., Page, T. J., Ivancic, M. T., & O'Brien, S. (1986). Analysis of environmental determinants of aggression and disruption in mentally retarded children. *Applied Research in Mental Retardation, 7*(2), 203–221.

McCord, B. F., Iwata, B. A., Galensky, T. L., Ellingston, S. A., & Thomsaon, R. J. (2001). Functional analysis and treatment of problem behavior evoked by noise. *Journal of Applied Behavior Analysis, 34*, 447–462.

Meany-Daboul, M. G., Roscoe, E. M., Bourett, J. C., & Ahearn, W. H. (2007). A comparison of momentary time sampling and partial-interval recording for evaluating functional relations. *Journal of Applied Behavior Analysis, 40*(3), 501–514.

Moore, J. W., Mueller, M. M., Dubard, M., Roberts, D. S., & Sterling-Turner, H. E. (2002). The influence of therapist attention on self-injury during a tangible condition. *Journal of Applied Behavior Analysis, 35*(3), 283–286.

Mueller, M. M., Sterling-Turner, H. E., & Moore, J. W. (2005). Towards developing a classroom-based functional analysis condition to assess escape-to-attention as a variable maintaining problem behavior. *School Psychology Review, 34*(3), 425–431.

Piazza, C. C., Bowman, L. G., Contrucci, S. A., Delia, M. D., Adelinis, J. D., & Goh, H. L. (1999). An evaluation of the properties of attention as reinforcement for destructive and appropriate behavior. *Journal of Applied Behavior Analysis, 32*(4), 437–449.

Querim, A. C., Iwata, B. A., Roscoe, E. M., Schliehenmeyer, K. J., Ortega, J. V., & Hurl, K. E. (2013). Functional analysis screening for problem behavior maintained by automatic reinforcement. *Journal of Applied Behavior Analysis, 46*, 47–60.

Rapp, J. T., Carroll, R. A., Strangeland, L., Swanson, G., & Higgins, W. J. (2011). A comparison of reliability measures for continuous and discontinuous recording methods: Inflated agreement scores with partial interval recording and momentary time sampling for duration events. *Behavior Modification*, 35(4), 389−402.

Rapp, J. T., Colby-Dirksen, A. M., Michalski, D. N., Carroll, R. A., & Lindenberg, A. M. (2008). Detecting changes in simulated events using partial-interval recording and momentary time sampling. *Behavioral Interventions*, 23, 237−269.

Roscoe, E. M., Rooker, G. W., Pence, S. T., Longworth, L. J., & Zarcone, J. (2009). Assessing the utility of a demand assessment for functional analysis. *Journal of Applied Behavior Analysis*, 42, 819−825.

Schaefer, H. H. (1970). Self-injurious behavior: Shaping 'head-banging' in monkeys. *Journal of Applied Behavior Analysis*, 3, 111−116.

Sellers, T. P., Alai-Rosales, S., & MacDonald, R. P. F. (2016). Taking full responsibility: The ethics of supervision in behavior analytic practice. *Behavior Analysis in Practice*, 4, 299−308.

Sellers, T. P., Valentino, A. L., & LeBlanc, L. A. (2016). Recommended practices for individual supervision of aspiring behavior analysts. *Behavior Analysis in Practice*, 9, 274−286.

Taylor, J. C., Sisson, L. A., McKelvey, J. L., & Trefelner, M. F. (1993). Situation specificity in attention-seeking problem behavior: A case study. *Behavior Modification*, 17(4), 474−497.

Thomason-Sassi, J. L., Iwata, B. A., Neidert, P. L., & Roscoe, E. M. (2011). Response latency as an index of response strength during functional analyses of problem behavior. *Journal of Applied Behavior Analysis*, 44, 51−67.

Turner, L. B. (2017). Behavior analytic supervision. In J. K. Luiselli (Ed.), *Applied behavior analysis advanced guidebook: A manual for professional practice* (pp. 3−20). New York: Elsevier-Academic Press.

Turner, L. P., Fischer, A. J., & Luiselli, J. K. (2016). Towards a competency-based, ethical, and socially valid approach to supervision of applied behavior analytic trainees. *Behavior Analysis in Practice*, 9, 287−298.

Valentino, A. L., LeBlanc, L. A., & Sellers, T. P. (2016). The benefits of group supervision and recommended structure for implementation. *Behavior Analysis in Practice*, 9, 320−328.

Vollmer, T. R., Marcus, B. A., Ringdahl, J. E., & Roane, H. S. (1995). Progressing from brief assessments to extended functional analyses in the evaluation of aberrant behavior. *Journal of Applied Behavior Analysis*, 28, 561−576.

FURTHER READING

Betz, A., & Fisher, W. W. (2011). Functional analysis: History and methods. In W. W. Fisher, C. C. Piazza, & H. S. Roane (Eds.), *Handbook of applied behavior analysis* (pp. 206−225). New York: Guilford.

Call, N. A., Scheithauer, M. C., & Mevers, J. L. (2017). Functional behavioral assessments. In J. K. Luiselli (Ed.), *Applied behavior analysis advanced guidebook: A manual for professional practice* (pp. 41−72). New York: Academic Press.

Carr, E. G., & Durand, V. M. (1985). Reducing behavior problems through functional communication training. *Journal of Applied Behavior Analysis*, 18, 111−126. Available from https://doi.org/10.1901/jaba.1985.18-111.

Fong, E. H., Catagnus, R. M., Broadhead, M. T., Quigley, S., & Field, S. (2016). Developing the cultural awareness skill of behavior analysts. *Behavior Analysis in Practice*, 9, 84−94.

Hagopian, L. P., Rooker, G. W., Jessel, J., & DeLeon, I. G. (2013). Initial functional analysis outcomes and modifications in pursuit of differentiation: A summary of 176 inpatient cases. *Journal of Applied Behavior Analysis*, 46, 88−100. Available from https://doi.org/10.1002/jaba.25.

Kazdin, A. E. (2013). *Behavior modification in applied settings* (7th ed.). Long Grove, IL: Wavland Press, Inc.

Lalli, J. S., Livezey, K., & Kates, K. (1996). Functional analysis and treatment of eye poking with response blocking. *Journal of Applied Behavior Analysis, 29*(1), 129–132.

Miltenberger, R. G. (2016). *Behavior modification: Principles and procedures* (5th ed.). Belmont, CA: Wardworth Publishing.

Najdowski, A. C., Wallace, M. D., Ellsworth, C. L., MacAleese, A. N., & Cleveland, J. M. (2008). Functional analyses and treatment of precursor behavior. *Journal of Applied Behavior Analysis, 41*(1), 97.

Northup, J., Wacker, D., Sasso, G., Steege, M., Cigrand, K., Cook, J., & DeRaad, A. (1991). A brief functional analysis of aggressive and alternative behavior in an outclinic setting. *Journal of Applied Behavior Analysis, 24*(3), 509–522.

Ringdahl, J. E., & Sellers, J. A. (2000). The effects of different adults as therapists during functional analyses. *Journal of Applied Behavior Analysis, 33*, 247–250. Available from https://doi.org/10.1901/jaba.2000.33-247.

Sigafoos, J., & Saggers, E. (1995). A discrete-trial approach to the functional analysis of aggressive behaviour in two boys with autism. *Journal of Intellectual and Developmental Disability, 20*(4), 287–297.

Smith, R. G., & Churchill, R. M. (2002). Identification of environmental determinants of behavior disorders through functional analysis of precursor behaviors. *Journal of Applied Behavior Analysis, 35*(2), 125–136.

Thompson, R. H., & Iwata, B. A. (2005). A review of reinforcement control procedures. *Journal of Applied Behavior Analysis, 38*(2), 257–278.

Tiger, J. H., Hanley, G. P., & Bessette, K. K. (2006). Incorporating descriptive assessment outcomes into the design of functional analysis: A case example. *Education and Treatment of Children, 29*, 107–124.

Wallace, M. D., & Iwata, B. A. (1999). Effects of session duration on functional analysis outcomes. *Journal of Applied Behavior Analysis, 32*, 175–183. Available from https://doi.org/10.1901/jaba.1999.32-175.

INDEX

Note: Page numbers followed by "*f*" refer to figures.

A
ABAB design, 59
Abolishing operations, 19–20, 25
Alone condition, 15–16, 23–24, 116–117
Alone session, conducting, 24
Attention condition, 15–16, 19–20, 29, 40–41, 64–65, 103–106, 114–115
   FA script for, 12*f*
   standard FA condition feedback form, 14*f*
Attention extinction, 2
Automatically maintained behavior, 25
Automatic negative reinforcement contingency, 17
Automatic positive reinforcement contingency, 16
Aversive events, 2, 15–16, 41

B
Baseline logic, 98–100
Behavior analysts, 2, 6–7
Behavior analytic practice, 1, 4–5, 7

C
Challenging behavior, 1–3, 6, 9–10, 15–16, 23, 36–37, 40–46, 59–60, 64–66, 101
Children and adults, conducting FA sessions with, 27
   practicing standard FA sessions with children and adults, 28–31
      adapting and selecting standard FA conditions for assessment, 28–29
      determining sequence of sessions, 29
      determining therapists for sessions, 30
      obtaining consent, 30–31
      risk prevention guidelines, 31
      selection of materials, 29–30
      session duration, 29
      supervised implementation of FA sessions, 31
   reproducible figures and forms, 31–37
      consent for functional analysis, 36–37
   training procedures, 27–28
      criterion to pass Level 2, 28
      training steps for Level 2, 28
Comprehensive training, 3, 5
Continuous recording methods, 55
Control phase, 59, 103–105

D
Data collection tools, 36
Demand, 22
Descriptive analysis, 36–37, 60
Differential reinforcement of other behavior (DRO) conditions, 42–43
Discontinuous measurement systems, 55, 58
Divided attention condition, 39–41
Duration, 57
   calculating estimated frequency and, 58–59

E
Environmental arrangement, 19–20
Environmental variables, 1–2
Escape condition, 9, 15–16, 22
   conducting, 22–23
   FA script for, 12*f*
   standard FA condition feedback form, 15*f*
Establishing operation (EO), 19–20, 29–30, 117
Estimated frequency and duration, calculating, 58–59
Experimental designs, 59–60
   multielement design, 60
   reversal design, 59–60
Experimental evaluations, 1
Extended alone/ignore condition, 66–67

F
Foundational skills, 27–28, 56
Frequency, 57–58
Functional behavior assessments (FBAs), 44
Functional communication response (FCR), 4

G
Graphing, 85–86
   reproducible figures for, 87

Graph interpretation, 88–108
　baseline logic–reversal designs, 98–106
　experimental control–multielement graphs, 106–108
　reproducible figures for, 109
　visual analysis, 90–98

H
Historical overview, of FA, 1–2

I
Idiosyncratic variables, 44, 60–61
Ignore condition, additional considerations for, 24–25
Individualization, 4–5
Interview-informed synthesized contingency analysis (IISCA), 67

K
Knuckle-cracking behavior, 17–18

L
Latency, 58
Latency-based FA, 4, 6
Latency functional analysis, 62–63
Level, determination of, 98
Level 2 functional analysis feedback forms, 28

M
Measurement, 56–59
　calculating estimated frequency and duration, 58–59
　discontinuous measurement systems, 58
　duration, 57
　frequency, 57
　latency, 58
　target behaviour, selecting, 56–57
Medical considerations, 6
Medical personnel, 3, 6, 31
Medical risk, 6
Methodology, 60–67
　extended alone/ignore condition, 66–67
　interview-informed synthesized contingency analysis (IISCA), 67
　latency functional analysis, 62–63
　precursor functional analysis, 63–64
　single-function functional analysis, 61–62
　standard functional analysis, 60–61
　trial-based functional analysis, 64–66
Momentary time sampling (MTS), 58–59
Motivating operation (MO), 19–20

Multielement design, 60–62
Multiple functions, 43, 60–61, 108
Multitier training process, 37–38

N
Negative-reinforcement contingency, 40–41, 45
　control condition for, 46–47
Noncontingent negative-reinforcement, 46–47
Noncontingent reinforcement (NCR), 45–46
Nontarget problem behavior, 21

O
Overarching themes, 3

P
Partial interval recording (PIR), 58–59
Peer interaction, 1–2
Performance data, 9–10
Play condition, 15–16, 25, 99–101
　FA script for, 13f
　standard FA condition feedback form, 16f
Play session, conducting, 25
Portfolio for conducting functional analysis, 123, 125, 130f
Portfolio scoring sheet, 125, 136f
Positive-reinforcement contingency, 40–41, 45
Postanalysis reporting form, 131f
Postanalysis training form, 124–125
Precursor functional analysis, 63–64
Prediction, 99–100
Problem behavior, 17, 19–21, 24–25, 28, 30, 37–38, 96–98, 108, 114–118

R
Reinforcement, automatic, 23–24
Replication, 99–100, 105–106
Reversal design, 59–62, 98–99, 116
Round robin activity, 9–10
　data sheet for, 10, 11f

S
Safety considerations, 4–5
Seasonal variations, 6
Selecting target behavior, 56–57
Self-injurious behavior (SIB), 21, 41, 56–57, 114–115
Sensory attenuation, 17
Session data, 57
Simulated condition feedback forms, 10

Simulated conditions, performance summary sheet for, 10–13
Single-case experimental design, 59
Single-function functional analysis, 61–62
Single-function test–control method, 61
Social avoidance condition, 39–40, 116
Standard functional analysis, 60–61
Standard functional analysis conditions, extending, 39
  reproducible figures and forms, 47–53
  training procedures, 39–40
    criteria to pass Level 3, 40
    training steps for Level 3, 39–40
  unique functional analysis conditions, developing, 40–47
    control condition for negative-reinforcement contingency, 46–47
    creating conditions, 45–46
    developing unique test and control conditions, 44
    different contexts/consequences, 43
    divided attention, 40–41
    EOs/consequences, 44–45
    multiple functions, 43
    paired consequences, 43
    screening for automatic reinforcement, 42
    variations of attention, 41
    variations of escape, 41–42
    variations to control session, 42–43
Standard functional analysis methodology, 3
Standard functional analysis sessions, conducting, 9, 15–25
  alone session, conducting, 24
  attention condition, 19–20
  automatic negative example, 17–18
  automatic positive example, 18–19
  demand, 22
  escape condition, conducting, 22–23
  functions of behavior, 16–17
  ignore condition, additional considerations for, 24–25
  motivating operations example, 20–21
  play (control) condition, 25
  play session, conducting, 25
  reinforcement, automatic, 23–24
  reproducible figures and forms, 25
  tangible condition, 20
    conducting, 21
    managing additional behaviors in, 21–22
  training procedures, s0010
    criteria to pass level 2, 14
    training steps for level 2, 10–14
Supervising caseloads, 125

Supervision, 3, 5
Supervision and mentoring, 123
  reproducible figures and forms, 126–135
  training procedures, 123–125
    criteria to pass Level 6, 125
    training steps for Level 6, 125

T

Tangible condition, 20, 28
  conducting, 21
  FA script for, 13f
  managing additional behaviors in, 21–22
  standard FA condition feedback form, 17f
Tangible items, 20–22, 43
Target behavior, 3–4, 9–10, 21–23, 28–29, 37, 45–46, 62–65, 67
Target problem behavior, 21
Target response, 23, 25, 95
Test phase, 59
Therapist differences, 30
Trainees, 9, 27–29, 39, 56, 79, 123–124
  competence, 31
  supervision, 31
Trainers, 3, 5–6, 9, 27, 125
Training considerations, 5
Training curriculum, 14, 27, 123
Training procedures, 9–14, 27–28, 39–40, 55–56, 79–84, 123–125
  criteria to pass Level 2, 14, 28
  criteria to pass Level 3, 40
  criteria to pass Level 6, 125
  criterion to pass Level 4, 56
  training steps for Level 2, 10–14, 28
  training steps for Level 3, 39–40
  training steps for Level 4, 56
  training steps for Level 6, 82–84, 125
    criteria to pass Level 5, 84
    graphing, 82–83
    graph interpretation, 83
    undifferentiated data, 83–84
Training-simulated conditions, task analysis for, 10–13
Trend, 96–98
Trial-based functional analysis, 64–66

U

Undifferentiated data, managing, 110–118
  addressing carryover effects, 115–116
  addressing challenges with discrimination, 115
  addressing low and undifferentiated data, 117

Undifferentiated data, managing (*Continued*)
  addressing potential automatic reinforcement, 116–117
  automatic reinforcement, 115
  carryover effects, 114–115
  failure to discriminate between conditions, 114
  gathering additional information, 117–118
  reproducible figures for, 118–121

V

Verification, 99–100, 103–105